CELIBACY FOR OUR TIMES

Religious Experience Series

Edward J. Malatesta, S.J., General Editor

Religious Experience Series No. 7

CELIBACY
FOR OUR TIMES

YVES RAGUIN SJ

Translated by
SISTER MARY HUMBERT KENNEDY O.P.

ANTHONY CLARKE
WHEATHAMPSTEAD, HERTFORDSHIRE

Celibacy For Our Times is the English translation of *Célibat pour Notre Temps*, published originally by Vie Chretienne, Paris.

This edition first published 1975
ANTHONY CLARKE BOOKS
Wheathampstead, Hertfordshire, England
also published in U.S.A. by Abbey Press, St. Meinrad, Indiana
All rights reserved

Reprinted 1978

ISBN 0 85650 031 3
ISSN 0305-3687

MADE AND PRINTED IN GREAT BRITAIN BY CHAPEL RIVER PRESS, ANDOVER, HAMPSHIRE

Contents

Introduction

The title of this book is an answer, not a question, because there is a celibacy for our times. The recent debate is the final stage in a quest that goes back, not to Vatican II, but to the beginnings of Christianity and indeed to before that time. Ever since the Creator-creature relationship stirred man's consciousness, the question has been posed. We have only to study the history of the great religious movements to be aware of this. The question was a simple one: Is there a search for and an encounter with God which may entail the sacrifice of marriage? And the answer was "Yes." That is the reason why, in the case of all the major religions, there have been men and women who, in order to find God more truly, renounced not only marriage but every kind of sexual union. If, then, every age has produced men and women who have seen fit to renounce such relationships the better to find God, our age can and ought to have its witnesses; and that is the reason why I entitled this booklet *Celibacy for Our Times.*

In this perspective, celibacy and virginity take on a new meaning and open up to man new horizons. However, many are of the opinion that the rediscovery of the grandeur of marriage as a way to God will render superfluous the celibate way of life. They are making a great mistake. In fact, the rediscovery of marriage is due in large part to the aspirations of those who have renounced it, and this discovery of the spiritual depths of conjugal intimacy has given Christians a new insight into the meaning of virginity.

We are creatures of history, and in the historical context no

1

moment is definitive. Rather it is constantly on the alert for the moment which will follow and surpass it. What is more, it prepares for that moment and longs for it. Nothing is definitive but that which transcends history and that which in history, symbolizes, expresses, or heralds that world beyond. Now celibacy and virginity belong to this order. Like marriage, they are lived out in human history with its trials and sorrows, while at the same time prefiguring a state which transcends history.

The debate in recent years on priestly celibacy makes the problem intensely actual. Not that celibacy in itself is being questioned; the debate revolves rather around its link to the priesthood. I have no intention here of entering into that debate. The Church could very well decide one day to have married priests just as she has opted for a celibate clergy. The reason for her decision could be found both in the pragmatic and in the spiritual or theological order.

What is more serious, it seems to me, is that the press, taking the debate into its own hands, has amplified and orchestrated it, often with disastrous results, because those who manage to shout loudest, and who have the largest audiences, are usually those for whom celibacy has lost all meaning. On the other hand, those who remain faithful are often silent persons whom God's love consumes, but who have no words to speak that love.

Am I mistaken in presuming that I can lend a voice to the silent witness of millions who are celibate for the sake of the Lord and for His Kingdom? Some accept being misunderstood —they are strong enough for that—but how many lose their balance when it is suggested to them that they are not normal, that they have no idea of what it is to love, that they are segregated from society, that they are living outside the human condition, and so on.

Sometimes I am inclined to think that those who launch their attack against the celibate state are persons who themselves have achieved happiness neither in celibacy nor in marriage, and who reconcile themselves in this way to their own particular failure. On the contrary, those who are happy in their state of life assume that others are likewise happy in theirs. This is the spirit in which I should like to present these reflections.

In 1967, I wrote an essay which I entitled "The Present-Day Value of Celibacy and Virginity." That essay was never published. The present text is a rewrite. Since 1967, I have had ample opportunity to think the problem over, as well as to live more deliberately my own consecration, while at the same time realizing what it represented for those men and women who are my close friends. What I write here, therefore, is not the fabric of a dream, but a lived reality.

The wonderful thing about celibacy—besides the hundred and one other aspects I shall deal with—is the freedom of heart it can offer. In the radiance of God's love, it dilates human intimacy to such a degree that it is with difficulty that one conceives of the possibility of such relationships. At the same time, it liberates the individual for tasks which demand that total gift of self which is beyond any price.

How many dedicated lives have gone into the composition of this booklet I cannot guess. Hundreds have created its atmosphere. A more restricted number provided material for the more fundamental chapters. Certain paragraphs, certain phrases, remind me of a face, a spoken word, an encounter.

This book is not, then, a mere dream, but the echo of lives lived in our own day and in every corner of the globe.

Yves Raguin, S.J.
Chang hua (Taiwan),
27 December 1971.

Part One

The Charism
of Celibacy

Chapter 1

"We Have Believed In Love"

Why do certain men and women renounce marriage? If one were to put that question to those who have renounced it within Christianity, the reply would be unanimous: "For His sake, for Christ."

For it is precisely in order to exploit life to the full that boys and girls, on its very threshold, prefer to choose, as the immediate and avowed object of their love, Him whom we call God, or in more concrete terms, God incarnate—Christ. But how can this be possible? Possible or impossible, the fact remains. To the question: "Who is going to share your life?" the reply: "Christ. It is He whom I love. To Him I have dedicated my life. Night and day. He it is who will be the object of my innermost thoughts. When you are in the company of him or her whom you love, I shall be apparently in nobody's company. I shall be alone, and you will be sorry for me. But don't be sorry. In Him, by Him, and with Him, I have encountered love. With St. John I can say that I have believed in love. Just as I believe in your love, believe me that I too know love's meaning."

They will not say: "If I have dedicated my life to God, it is because I am frightened of marriage and should like to live a peaceful life within a community." Perhaps considerations of that nature entered into the decision, but they were of secondary importance. One could, in fact, put together all the why's and wherefore's, and yet they would never outweigh the chief reason, namely, that it is for Him, for Christ, that they have made the sacrifice, she of this attractive young boy, strong and capable of loving, he of this affectionate young girl, intelligent and fresh as an April day.

At the decisive moment, one does not choose against a particular love, but for another love. This is what is involved in one's choice, when it is a question of living out one's entire existence in the light of a unique decision. However, when a boy hesitates between several girls, it is not always obvious that the girl he loves best is the one he will choose. He may perhaps decide to marry a girl he loves less deeply, because he was imprudent in his relationship with her, and thus she retains a hold on him. There is not much point in dwelling here on exceptional cases, because in the ordinary run of things one chooses for love and not against it. Both the boy and the girl will do their utmost to choose the person they love. It is inevitable, however, that there will be failures in marriage, badly matched couples, lack of harmony between persons, and, consequently, failures in love. Human life is not always what we would wish it to be. One has to live it as it is, and derive from it the best one can. A woman surrenders herself to a man when she is convinced that she is loved, or in order to have that certitude. Quite frequently, she gives herself because she is afraid of losing a particular partner, or, again, because she wants to have a child. Such are life's realities; it would be naive, to say the least, were one to think that every encounter between man and woman is a true love encounter.

This is why in the case of the majority of vocations to celibacy, alongside love to God, other factors—some happy, some unhappy—are also found. It is the misery, just as much as the grandeur of human love, that opens one's eyes to the unique reality of divine love. A large percentage of those who choose celibacy are persons endowed with exquisite sensibility, who are capable of an extraordinary love, but who for that very reason in a certain sense fear the daily human condition. Must we blame them if they seek to be freed from it? In Japan, for example, the lot reserved to women inside marriage orients toward religious life a considerable number of young girls who in another social context would have made admirable wives. Thus we see that a fear of certain realities and a desire to be freed from them may motivate a vocation. But in the long run, what clinches the choice is the possibility of loving Him of whom it can be said that He will be faithful during life, until death, and throughout eternity.

The choice of celibacy for Christ and for the Kingdom is neither a no to human love nor even a refusal of its inevitable suffering, but a yes to "infinite love." It is also a yes, timid at first, perhaps, to a love that is human, liberated it is true from the imperatives of the flesh, but just as true, as deep, and as ardent as the most perfect of human loves. The liberty of heart which celibacy ought to give, opens up, in fact, enormous perspectives. The love which God bears us and that which we offer Him dilates the human heart to divine capacities of loving and being loved.

When a young man or a young girl informs his or her parents of a decision to live a celibate life, the family is quite often embarrassed when it comes to telling their friends. They will say: "You know it's his (her) idea." Obviously, neither the boy nor the girl is going to speak about what has taken place in the secret recesses of the heart. They are afraid of being misunderstood or, worse still, of being mocked. But to those in whom they have confidence, they will reveal all.

Slowly, year after year, they discovered that somebody loved them: Jesus Christ. He it was who invited them into His intimacy, just as He attracted John, Andrew, Peter, and the rest. Between them, a dialogue was begun; a friendship was slowly born which, little by little, revealed itself as a deep love. Sometimes the encounter is sudden, like a flash; sometimes it is a slow discovery. But in every case, Christ is living, demanding time, attention, life, one's very being even. And after many years, looking back on their lives, they can still say: "We have believed in love."

Chapter 2

Saying Yes to Love

Love resides either on the surface or in the depth of our being. Some "loves" scarcely go beyond the biological, but there are others which absorb a whole being and are its very life. Love measures itself by the depth of a relationship, and so it takes a long time to arrive at the genuine thing, which can only develop in a kind of death to the self. It is easy to say yes to superficial love, but to say yes to love which gives all and demands all is beyond the capacity of many human beings.

Such a yes supposes certitude. It follows, then, that one must be able to make an act of total faith in the other, or at least an act of confidence which will permit the first love experience to manifest itself. Love, however, reveals itself as a fathomless abyss. To love someone is to experience intense pleasure, but also intense suffering . . . because of oneself, because of the other, or because of both simultaneously. Love is an interchange of joy, doubled and redoubled, a gift received which regives itself until nothing remains in the depths of one's person but a great emptiness which is, at the same time, the greatest plentitude a man can know.

So love is to say yes to another, to say yes not merely with the lips or even with the heart, but with one's whole being. The yes is uttered before the total giving, and yet it is the yes which guarantees the certainty of love. The experience of love in a bodily embrace gives new expression to the gift already offered.

11

Love resonates with a new harmony. The entire sensibility is called into play; love orchestrates on the body's lyre, is the harmony of the flesh, but the notes reverberate ceaselessly until they reach the depths of each being where already for a long time the reciprocal yes has prepared and given all. When the entire human being with its every fiber, when a total existence, moment by moment, has been integrated into that love uttered by the yes, love will have attained its perfection.

At certain times it happens that two persons in love are conscious neither of flesh nor of spirit, neither of heart nor of intellect; nothing seems to matter anymore but that wonderful reality that they are together, each in the presence of the other, with the other, in the other. Such a state is rare in day-to-day living, but it is realized often enough to give an understanding of what it is to love and to be loved . . . which in fact are one and the same. The yes uttered in response to love can become the reality of daily living.

The first response to love's initial stirrings cannot be as yet the yes which is entire giving and total confidence. As yet, it is little more than a timid acquiescence to the hope of a more intimate encounter. The journeying will be slow, perhaps even painful, for that yes can only be uttered in certitude. But one is never as sure of the other as one is of oneself, seeing that the other can only be known in the impression one receives. All this explains why it is characteristic of love to advance with extreme caution for fear of giving itself to one who is unworthy.

How long a time it takes before one can make a total act of faith in another person! The yes is uttered, and something is changed utterly. A door has been opened. "The door of my heart has been opened, and through that door, where until now I alone had entrance, another passes, alone or in my company. At other times when I am least expecting him, he comes, and without knocking, enters. He is there, having taken me unawares. Unawares yes, but only in a sense, for all the time my heart was waiting. And it was through the door of my heart that he made his entry. While I slept, he touched me gently with his hand; I trembled with joy and really knew then that

I loved him. Without hesitation, for there was no longer any reason to hesitate, I said yes to his love. I knew that he loved me and that I too loved him."

On such a note the Canticle of Canticles sings its love song ... divine love vibrating on human strings! Some are shocked to read such language in one of the books of the Bible, but how otherwise could love express itself if not in the language of lovers? The notion of God's love itself cannot be grasped unless it find some echo in my poor human heart. God plays His love song on the chords of a human harp, on chords which are taut, on an instrument of nerves and sinews and bones.

If, in order to know God's love, man had but the beautiful revelations of Christ and St. John, if he had only texts such as "God so loved the world as to give His only begotten Son" (Jn 3:16) ... "Having loved His own, He loved them unto the end" (Jn. 13:1 ... "God is love ..." (Jn. 4:8), this would hardly suffice to convince him of the value of celibacy as a response to God's love. What finally convinces men and women is that one day God manifests Himself to them personally and in such a manner that it is only by saying no to a love realizable in marriage that they can say yes to the love which He offers and which captivates their whole being.

Chapter 3

Divine Advances

Right from the beginning, God made love advances toward man. All of creation is a call to love, and man who cannot—or at least ought not—contemplate that creation without thinking of its Creator is well aware of this. There is that wonderful passage in Genesis where God gives Eve to Adam. Yahweh fashions a woman and brings her to Adam who cries out: "Here is bone of my bone and flesh of my flesh" (Genesis 2: 23). On seeing her, Adam discovers himself. In the contemplation of this being like himself, and yet so different, he discovers his own identity.

This is why in the normal run of things man has need of a woman to understand and realize himself. In the presence of this companion he discovers his most intimate self, just as she senses in her inmost being that she is understood and loved without measure unto perfect intimacy.

The Genesis narrative must be read in its totality. A human relationship of the kind described could have catastrophic consequences were it to sever the relationship—more fundamental still—which unites man to God. Nevertheless, in this man and in this woman, to whom He has communicated life, God reveals Himself by causing love to awaken in their hearts.

God's love for man spans Scripture from beginning to end. Over and over again in the Old Testament God expresses His love for His chosen people, for His dearly-cherished though often unfaithful bride. We tend to conceive of God's love in a very anthropomorphic fashion, but we have scarcely any alternative. God speaks in such a way that He will be understood by the entire human race, at first through human nature itself, then by means of the prophets, and finally by sending His Son who will reveal, that everything is created by love.

While exacting that we be perfect as His heavenly Father is perfect, Christ never claimed to found a sinless Church, a sort of club for the perfect, a spiritual elite. Nor did He preach flight from the human condition. That is why he never laid it down as an essential condition of discipleship that one renounce marriage and follow the way of consecrated chastity. One can just as well be a disciple of Jesus in married life. We have only to look at His presence at the wedding feast at Cana, and the miracle He accomplished there, to see His blessing on the ordinary state of human existence. On another occasion, Jesus reminds His listeners that a man and his wife form but one flesh (Mt. 19:5-6). He does not, then, situate perfection in the sacrifice of the bodily aspects of life, but in the spirit in which such realities are lived. This is what St. Paul meant when he said that the spirit must not come under the domination of the flesh.

And yet, Christ does not hesitate to propose another form of perfection: wife and family can be left for the sake of the kingdom of God (Lk. 18:29-30). On another occasion, in answer to those who criticized Him and His disciples for remaining celibate, His statement is unambiguous, "There are those who make themselves eunuchs for the sake of the kingdom of heaven. Let him who can understand, understand" (Mt. 19:12). Thus did Christ try to awaken the desire of a more direct response to divine love. Those who live their marriage in a truly religious perspective are well aware that their love is the sign of a still greater love. At times, in their mutual ecstasy, lovers seem to touch the source of their love which then reaches out beyond itself. In a common transport of love, the self and the other are lost in a love which is the source of all loves. The divine love is the ultimate revelation of Christ to man.

There exists, then, between God and man a love which does not pass through conjugal union, but which joins man to his Creator by way of celibacy and virginity. Many find it difficult to imagine that such a thing is possible, but the fact that it exists is proof of its possibility. God reveals Himself as the sole object of their love, and He does so by revealing that He is the ultimate source of all other loves. In the light of this reality there is no denial of the grandeur of human love; what happens simply is that the very source of love manifests Himself directly as He who loves and He whom one must love.

This is what John the beloved disciple certainly understood; it is what Mary Magdalen, with her affectionate heart, realized after having first passionately attached herself to the person of Jesus, the prophet.

Christ was so discreet in inviting man to lead a life of virginity that St. Paul was able to say that, on this topic, he had no positive teaching from the Lord. Yet Paul wished that others be like himself (1 Cor. 7:28). Thus we see how free is the call to perfect virginity in the mind of Christ and of St. Paul. In marriage, love for God grows in the love of one's partner, while at the same time revealing itself greater than that love. This is why God can ask that He be loved for Himself and in Himself. Such a request points to the way of celibacy and virginity.

Chapter 4

Why Celibacy?

If God can be found in marriage, why then celibacy? This is the question that many put both to themselves and to others. They have, in fact, the idea that the Church institutionalized celibacy out of a disdain for marriage; and they point the finger at God knows who, for dividing man and opposing flesh and spirit.

Now that we have rediscovered the true nature of man, now that human love has been restored to its rightful place and recognized as an authentic way to God, celibacy, they hold, has no longer any justification. Marriage is the normal state, and the love of God has no need for these "superior" Christians.

But if God can be found in marriage, it ought to be conceded that He can also be found in celibacy. Each man ought to be free to follow the road he wishes to follow. If I marry, it is because I can best realize my ideal that way; if I renounce marriage, it is because I have discovered a love to which I cannot relate fully except by remaining celibate.

As long as Christianity is Christianity, one cannot ignore the fact that Christ remained celibate and that His mother was a virgin. In His immediate entourage the "disciple whom Jesus loved" was a virgin, as was Joseph and John the Baptist. If in the Jewish mentality parenthood was the ideal, there was also a strong tradition in favor of celibacy, especially amongst the Essenes. Furthermore, Christ was to present consecrated celibacy as an ideal for those "able to understand."

In all the great religions, two traditions are to be found: one represented by a married clergy, in which the functional aspect predominates, the other by unmarried religious whose chief concern is the search for God by the way of contemplation. These traditions are also found in Christianity, which includes the Oriental and Protestant traditions. Now, while sexual union can be a means to God, it is also true that the more intimate approach to Him, be it ritual or not, is normally linked with celibacy and virginity, or at least with continence.

Such facts cannot be examined, unless in the depths of the human conscience there lies the conviction that the ultimate approach to God transcends the male-female relationship, a relationship which is, besides, imperfect and which does not lead to the final stage of the journey. It must in fact die, so that man can achieve perfect union with God.

One can express this in another way by saying that the deepest relationship that man can realize with his God is an act of virginity, a direct encounter, a union without any intermediacy. Such a relationship is a response to God's initial act whereby He called man into being and continues to communicate to him His life and His spirit, in a direct relationship which dispenses with all created mediation.

Human life fortunately comes to the aid of metaphysics! How many couples encounter God in a direct manner, which transcends their union and gives it depth. As intimacy grows between man and woman, they become more interiorly present to each other; and the source and ultimate meaning of their love becomes more transparent. They are carried along by a force greater than themselves, and realize that both individually and in their togetherness they are speechless with admiration before God, the origin of their life and the ideal of their love.

Thus they discover that ultimate love is inaccessible save by an act of pure virginity. Why not interpret thus Christ's words: "In the resurrection, they neither marry nor are given in marriage ... " (Mt. 22:30). Sexual union belongs to the human condition here below. In the next world it will be transcended. Those who were united in this world will be united also in the next, but in a way impossible to describe. Nevertheless, human experience can give us some idea of what this union will be like at the resurrection.

Each will experience a perfect union with those whom he loved in this world. At the same time, there will be between God and each person a relationship, direct, unique, and as complete as there could possibly be between God and His creation. It is then that married people will understand why others preferred to follow the way of perfect chastity in order to respond to Christ's love, and to be in this earthly existence the privileged witnesses of eternal life.

However, it would be wrong to view celibacy solely from an eschatological point of view as a sign of the times to come. For this future is already present in history. What will come "after," at the end of time, is already present as eternity in the heart of time and in the depths of each one's being.

Chapter 5

Eschatology at the Heart of Life

To give weight to the notion of celibacy, its eschatological aspect is often emphasized, namely, that the one who dedicates his or her virginity to God, witnesses to a future life, and is a reminder to those tempted to forget that in the next world there will be neither marrying nor giving in marriage, but that we shall be like the angels in heaven. Such testimony, however, is hardly convincing for one who here below has met the perfect husband or the ideal wife.

Every man seeks happiness, and since the beginnings of Christianity many have wished to store up treasures for themselves in heaven. Like wise businessmen, they have made sound investments. There is the danger, however, that such an attitude may give a gloomy color to existence in this world.

But there is a way to bring the life of the world-to-come right into the heart of this present life, since it exists there already. And this is precisely what a life consecrated to God ought to do. Before being a sign of the world-to-come, it is first and foremost a special sign of eternal life lived in time. This eternal life is hidden within us, there where God dwells and shares with us His own life. St. John expresses this reality in a wonderfully simple way: "Now we are the children of God, but we do not yet know what we shall be. Yet we know that when He manifests Himself we shall be like Him, for we shall see Him as He is" (1 Jn. 3:2). Now we are the children of God, and we know that we are loved by the Father who, with the Son and the Holy Spirit, dwells within us (see Jn. 14:23).

Such is the essential fact of the Christian life. Every Christian ought to live this divine life which is present within him, a life which is in fact his baptismal grace. There is only one Christ and one Christian grace. The grace of a priest or a religious is no different from the grace of other Christians. Nevertheless, the face remains that every grace is personal, because it is above all a relationship. That is why Christ says that only those whom He has called and who have answered that call can understand the meaning of consecrated celibacy.

Baptismal grace is given to all so that it may take root and grow either within marriage or in the celibate state. What finally determines the choice is the particular nuance of one's personal relationship to Christ. To grasp the significance of this relationship, one has only to open the Gospel to see how Christ enters into communion with each person He meets. Every time, He reveals a different aspect of the face of God.

When one day a particular individual is seized upon by God and feels himself called to a consecrated life, it is not primarily because he wants to witness to the world-to-come that he responds to God's invitation. The reason why young men or young women dedicate their virginity to God and vow themselves to His service in celibacy is that all of a sudden Christ entered into their lives, coming so close to them and manifesting His love in such a way that the force of that love swept away every other love dream they may have entertained.

The experience of this divine love is not always as vivid or as decisive, but its result is the same. Christ presents Himself as the friend who awaits an answer. Sometimes an answer is unnecessary because it is already present in the invitation. Sometimes again, there is a real uncertainty, even debate, and the answer is not always yes to the call of Christ. He who says yes to the divine invitation knows that he is choosing a state of life which is a sign of the world-to-come, but which is first of all, for him, a reality of this present time.

If his reply is affirmative, it is because he loves Christ as a brother, a friend, a dearly beloved. At times, he is conscious of the countenance of God as the master of life, and in this instance his decision may be colored by fear—fear of punishment because of possible sins, or fear of death. All these motivations may be fraught with illusions, but what is important here and now is that his decision to remain celibate is the consequence of an encounter between man and his God. In a spiritual experience, man became conscious of the divine will and replies to that will as he believes he ought to reply.

This is how vocations are decided. God comes into a person's life, directly by means of Christ, or through Mary's intermediary, or in some completely different way. He intervenes suddenly in a life, just as a young man or a young girl enters into another's life and awakens love. When God thus appears, there is no longer question of whether or not celibacy is a sign of the world-to-come, for it then appears as the necessary condition of a response to love's invitation. It is not love itself, but the expression and the sign of love.

Chapter 6

And for the Love
of Others

Celibacy is motivated first and foremost by a personal response to the love which God manifests to us; but there are several chords essential to the harmony of this motivation, for example, the gift of self to others. It is rare, indeed very rare, that God's love is discovered completely outside the desire to spend oneself for others.

When a young boy or girl experiences God's love, and I mean that love to which they can only respond by remaining celibate, two images present themselves. The first is that of a family they might found and whose happiness would be their happiness. Whether one likes it or not, this image evokes the idea of a cosy sheltered world where everybody loves everybody, but which is necessarily cut off to some extent from the rest of the world. Side by side with this comes another image: a life that is certainly not loveless, but which is wholly occupied with another love ... a life entirely consecrated to the Lord but open to the world and ready to transcend all its demands.

It appears to the young man or to the young girl that they would be freer to love and help others if they did not have a family their own. If in their childhood they have themselves

27

tasted the joys of family life, it will be an immense sacrifice for them to renounce the possibility of re-creating that happy atmosphere in a new family. If they have already known what deep friendship is, if they ever experienced the first stirrings of love, they will not say yes to Christ's love without real heart pangs. But that is all to the good, and the fact that they already know what love is will permit divine love to reveal itself far more truly.

This virginal love demands the sacrifice of some of the joys of human love, but in exacting this sacrifice God prepares witnesses with hearts as great as His own. Thus when one gives one's heart to God, one discovers that His heart is the rendez-vous of the entire human race.

There is, however, a temptation for the one who engages on the path of celibacy, and that is to allow the heart to close up. Worse still, there are some who think that, in order to love God, one must say no to all other loves. The truth is that he who understands something of God's love, and in whose heart divine love finds an echo, is not satisfied with loving God, but reaches out to all men as well.

Our life unfolds in history, and we discover reality according to our experience of it. When somebody first understands that God is calling him to His love, and service in a celibate life, the reaction is painful; and the heart suffers. We are, after all, human beings; and it is not easy to give up the perspective of a happy marriage and family. Neither is it romantic or sentimental to say that, while we rejoice at the thought of giving ourselves to God, we weep also at the thought that another kind of love must be transcended and passed by.

And yet, while renouncing the possibility of loving a particular man or woman, while sacrificing the joy of children to whom we would devote every minute of our lives, other possible gifts—and in infinite variety—present themselves. The discovery of God's love, while in a sense breaking our hearts, gives them a new dimension which puts us at the disposition of those who have need of us.

This gift of ourselves to others is so important that very

often it is the sole motive advanced for celibacy. How many are literally swept off their feet by God's love, responding to that love with every fiber of their being, and yet, through sheer modesty, are unable to reveal what has passed in the depths of their hearts. One does not voice such matters; they are too intimate for conversation. Who, for instance, would admit to having been smitten by Christ's love, who would admit to being ready to live solely because of Him and with Him and in Him, to say that His friendship was all-absorbing? Such things remain unexpressed. I have often heard people say: "Never could I talk to another about the love of God that I feel within me. Who would understand?" Some wait ten or twenty years before they can speak of that encounter with Christ which changed their lives. Having experienced love at such depths, how can they speak of it to anyone but the One who has awakened that love in their hearts?

There are in the world priests, religious, and lay people who hide their real vocation behind what they call "service to others," something which is easy to say. It is plain for all to see that their dedication is total, and they claim that here lies the essence of their vocation. That is true, but with exquisite delicacy they also hide the fact that the inspiration behind this gift of self was their unique love for Christ. There lies their secret; therein lies their treasure. If they do not speak about it, it is because they fear being misunderstood. There is always a tendency to sneer a little at people who believe in love to that extent—they are regarded as somewhat naive. In that case, the most naive of all was the Lord Himself who came into the world to tell us that He loves us.

But He wasn't so naive as one might think, this Jesus of Nazareth. He loved us unto the end, until His heart was completely emptied. More people than one might think, follow Him and love Him. They can say with St. John: "We have believed in love." Love of God and love of men, both are one: the two faces of the same love.

Chapter 7

Forever

The motives for which one assumes the celibate way of life are often very complex, and the decision is not always made for the best of reasons. When it is made for the reason already indicated, in response to God's love and as a gift of self to other, then there is every reason to suppose that the decision will remain firm, come what may. Motivations of this kind are in themselves so lofty and serious that he who so engages himself, considers himself irrevocably bound. It is the depth of the engagement that guarantees its continuity.

It is the very same in the case of human love. If it is superficial, and a mere attraction for another's charm, it will soon be in difficulties. If, on the other hand, it is genuine love for the other person, then no tempests can shake it. This is the love "strong as death" about which the Canticle speaks, a love that neither loss nor failure, neither evil nor sickness can destroy. It is solid as a rock, and like the diamond cannot be broken.

Astonishment is often great, both in Christian and in non-Christian circles, at the apparent facility with which priests and religious ask to be freed from their vows. Even those not hostile to the idea of a married clergy understand with difficulty how a contract vis-a-vis God and the Christian community can have less binding force than the marriage contract. It is useless to say that this is a different proposition. After all, a promise is a promise and a vow is a vow.

If we were married, some priests say, there would be no question of divorce, because one would respect the promise made to one's partner, especially if there were children; but in the case of a priest seeking laicization, consequences are not serious. Nevertheless, putting aside the effects that infidelity to a promise leaves in a man's heart, what about all those people for whom we are priests and who expect from us a service that only a priest can render? The world is full of lay persons; as for priests, whose privilege it is to be, in a sense, Jesus Christ among men, their numbers are decidedly smaller.

I am speaking here without laying the blame on anyone's shoulders. There are, I know, persons in impossible situations; and God is our soul judge, mine as well as theirs. But as a man, I base my reason on a human reality, in order to try to throw some light on the present confusion. If a priest who, for personal fulfillment, desires marriage, but ultimately renounces it because he is also aware of his responsibilities toward God's people, he will quite probably be accused of a want of sincerity, because his decision was motivated by his faith and not by his personal need. But if, on the other hand, he claims that he can no longer live his celibacy, which has lost all meaning for him, and that he wants to be a man like the rest; furthermore, if he leaves the priesthood in order to marry—all that is accepted as quite normal. It is easy to see, then, why so many married people who wish to separate, but who manage to continue living together for the simple reason that they made a promise to do so—until death—it is easy to see, I say, why such people feel resentment toward priests and religious who have no scruple about asking to be relieved from their promises.

If many marriages end in divorce, it is usually because they were hastily entered into. Now this is rarely so in the case either of religious profession or of priestly ordination. Consequently, it is hard for a priest to admit that he had not time to think things over. He might also conclude that he was led in a cloud of incense to a sort of dream-priesthood. But isn't all human life more or less like that? The moment one decides one's future—between seventeen and twenty-five is the period of one's life when it is easiest to take wing and follow a dream burgeoning in the mind or in the heart. Young priests and religious, like young married people, can bear witness to this fact. Love does not appear to deceive us, but to charm us into making a decision which will engage an entire life. In the case of celibacy, just as in the case of marriage, important decisions to be realized in full maturity are taken when the heart is afire with love and enthusiasm. If one forgets that, then both celibacy and marriage will end in disaster.

In each case, the operative word is "forever." It would be ever so much easier if we could straightaway enter eternity. But here below, "forever" means day after day in a life which is changing at every instant, in an existence where the personality is growing and identifying itself, where the feelings are being awakened unto self-discovery. Who knows what the feelings of my heart will be tomorrow or whether a happy encounter is not going to endanger my first love?

Thus we see the significance of the "forever" pronounced in the early twenties. If later on it is to be uttered with like sincerity—and it may happen that a husband will be tempted to go to bed with someone else's wife, or a priest to break his ordination promise—if this "forever" is to be uttered with the same sincerity as it was uttered in the twenties, it must have been pronounced day after day in the heart. Such a priest might say that at twenty he was ignorant of the force of human love. But who at twenty knows what is in store for him at forty? Here lies the human condition. This is the reason why in the case of celibacy, just as in that of marriage, promises are solemn. They ought, in normal conditions, to be inviolable forever.

Chapter 8

Without Having Really Desired It

The recent celibacy crisis shows that many who abandon their state never really wished to enter upon it. Celibacy was but one of the many conditions required for the priesthood or for entry into religious life, the ideal of which appeared attractive. For such persons, celibacy was one of the conditions of a life given to the service of God and of others. True, they saw the sacrifice it would entail; but since so many others had trodden the same route, they thought that all would be well for them too.

In a Christian environment great honor is attached to the priesthood or to religious profession. They are states of life to be envied for the prestige they confer and sometimes also for the relative ease they assure. Thus it happens that many arrive at ordination without quite knowing how they got there. They chose the priesthood and had no reason for not persevering in it. Also, a certain human respect and family pride, added to other motivations, safeguarded their celibacy.

In traditional Christianity, it was relatively easy to be a good priest. There was always more than enough work to do. Besides, people held the priesthood in high esteem, and its members were consequently sustained in their efforts—sometimes heroic efforts—to remain faithful. Nevertheless, celibacy was for some a necessary evil, and many compensated in the strictest secrecy for what they could abstain from only with the greatest difficulty.

Celibacy is possible and even relatively easy when one is truly sustained by the friendship of others with the same ideal, and when one enjoys the esteem of the Christian community. Some, it is true, jog along as best they can; but others travel joyfully with great ease and with great liberty. That there are weaknesses and lapses—and who can deny it?—tarnishes not a whit the grandeur of the ideal.

The essential is not to be free of difficulties, but to face them and to know whether or not one can hope to surmount them. To desire celibacy in all sincerity is to desire it existentially, that is, in a flesh-and-blood existence. A young man may have difficulty in remaining chaste, but at the same time know that if he wishes to remain so, and if he acts as he ought, then he will emerge victorious. In spite of risks which the future inevitably entails, a young man or a young woman can, at the moment of choice, be sure of God's call, and be convinced after many years of experience that they should engage themselves definitively in their vocation.

It is all too easy to say that circumstances alter. Of course they do, but it is precisely a proof of one's maturity to be able to steer a steady course, through the fluctuations of circumstances, toward that which surpasses them. When a young man marries, he ought to face the fact that he will meet girls who are more beautiful, more intelligent, and more attractive than the one he has chosen. When a young man engages in the celibate life, he should know that later on—perhaps in the forties—he will feel the need of a female presence in his life. Likewise women-religious, after years of peace in this regard, are suddenly overcome by a burning desire to love and be loved.

If such men and women have not really desired celibacy as a means of union with Christ, with the Church, with truth and with love, they will be tempted at the moment of trial to say:

"I never really meant to deprive myself so radically or to experience such solitude." And so great will be their desire to prove to themselves and to show others that they are truly men and women that celibacy will appear to them as something imposed from outside. They will hold it against the Church for having spoiled their lives in preventing them from being like everyone else. "If that's what celibacy is," they say, "then it's not what we wanted."

In a sense they are right; for in the eyes of Christ, of the Church, of the saints, and of those who know, celibacy is not that at all. Who ever would desire celibacy if it were but solitude, lack of affection, dryness of heart, and a negation of life? If celibacy appears thus, it is because nothing remains of it but the empty shell, the legal formula which states that a priest or male religious shall remain wifeless and that a woman religious shall not take a husband. Nobody could be inspired to choose such a celibacy!

But how does one arrive at the stage of seeing in a celibate life nothing more than its prohibitions and its limitations, in other words, its negative aspect merely? It seems to me that the reason lies in the fact that at the beginning the candidate for celibacy did not choose what lies at its heart, namely, love, that special love which eclipses and therefore rules out conjugal love. Instead, celibacy was accepted as part and parcel of the contract which one had to sign if one wished to be a priest or a member of a religious community.

Perhaps in the beginning, one did say a wholehearted yes to love, but afterwards forgot to cultivate it. Love of God demands the same attentions as does human love. At the moment of solemn promise, one is as the bride on the eve of her marriage. Love has given all, but the life of love is only beginning. As the seasons come and go, year by year, it must, like the young sapling, plunge its roots ever more deeply in the soil and spread out its branches in all directions.

Chapter 9

Charism and Institution

If priests renouncing celibacy were to be found in the ranks of the secular clergy only, one might say that the link between celibacy and the priesthood is the cause of the recent turmoil. In reality the malaise goes deeper. Far too many men religious, secular priests, and Sisters have lost the sense of total dedication to God, for they have allowed their faith to weaken. Only faith, indeed only faith with a particular nuance, can assure fidelity to Christ in the celibate state.

To maintain that the root of the evil lies in the Church's decision to link celibacy with the priesthood is to turn attention away from the real problem. Christ Himself went to the heart of the matter when He said there are those who have made themselves eunuchs for the kingdom of heaven. Not everyone can understand this. And we must add, as in the case of every action necessitating faith, that we cannot really understand except when we ourselves become involved. Nothing short of the genuine living of a celibate life for Christ will reveal its totality, for it is in the living of it that one discovers its deepest meaning.

Here the Church intervenes, for her faith is open to a wider experience than that of each Christian in particular. Thus she gives to those desiring to consecrate themselves to God, helps and assurances. This in itself creates problems, for the Church is always tempted to be excessively vigilant in regard to promises, fidelity to which she has guaranteed.

It is easy to blame the Church for having imposed rules and set up safeguards which have proved inefficacious. However, all the blame must not be laid at her doors, for has she not at the same time placed alongside her guarantee the treasures of her tradition, of her interior life, indeed of Christ Himself. Those, then, who have abandoned their vocation ought first of all to ask themselves if they have been faithful to the Lord's call, and if they have done their level best to protect a vocation to which they should have been faithful and which should have developed without any pressures from others. Such a question can only be answered in the depths of one's heart in all sincerity, before Christ Himself.

Must celibacy then be imposed on priests? If the priesthood is regarded as nothing more than a simple service to the Christian community, then it becomes more and more difficult to see how celibacy can be demanded for such a ministry. Still, the Church can, as she has done throughout the centuries, and in spite of all good reasons to the contrary, exact celibacy for her priests.

There are no theological or traditional reasons which determine absolutely that priests be celibate. While one can point to the ancient tradition of celibacy in the Church, one can also point to the still more ancient tradition of a married clergy; and this seems to be an excellent argument in favor of a change in legislation. But going still farther back, we find ourselves face to face with Christ and His apostles. Now Christ was certainly not married. He did not institute the priesthood in the sense we understand it today. He chose apostles; and even though some of them were married when Christ called them, it is very likely that, after their election, all chose to remain celibate for the Kingdom. As for St. Paul, he states that on that issue he has no clear precept from the Lord; and he hands over the care of the churches both to married and to unmarried men. But he wishes that all remain as he is himself, and it is for these reasons that it is impossible to create a theological link between celibacy and the priesthood. However, the fact that the Church has throughout history and in the wake of violent quarrels forbidden her priests to marry is already a strong argument in favor of ecclesiastical celibacy.

Besides, the reintroduction of a married clergy for practical reasons—as is already proposed—in countries where there are few priests is a poor solution in the eye of those who see the problem in depth.

What is necessary is that theologians and spiritually minded people get to work on the problem, for it seems that such questions are not the prerogative of a synod of bishops, more preoccupied with administration and pastoral life. The Church as a whole must decide what powers Christ has confided to her, and then to whom she will delegate those powers. She could decide to entrust some of her mission to celibates and some to married people. The question that interests us here is whether she should confide to married or to unmarried men the powers which she has up to this point entrusted to the priest. It would be premature to answer that question now, because the Church cannot make a decision until, in the light of the Holy Spirit, the solution to the question becomes "evident."

Part Two

The Experience
of Celibacy

Chapter 10

"I Will Espouse Thee in Faith"

Divine love and human love elicit in the heart the same emotions, and the feelings vibrate to the touch of God's love as they do to the deepest stirrings of human affection. Both loves play on the same instrument; but in the case of divine love, the quality of the resonance gives one to understand that it comes from a distance, and that being so, the vibration is deeper.

When God's call comes simultaneously with the awakening of human love, the chances appear unequal; and yet they are not so. It is, in fact, possible to be so sure of God's love that no human love can outrival it.

Whatever be the nature of the experience that leads me to opt for celibacy, that option is always made in faith. Even when God gives the soul an experience of His love that transports it outside itself, this union is effected in faith. The yes in itself is an act of faith; love is perceived, received, and lived only in a faith context.

Many have vowed their lives to God in celibacy without even having thought about the problem of loving. They followed that path because they were convinced that God was calling them; because they were aware that God's Church was

45

in need of priests, Sisters, and Brothers; because the Church is in constant need of missionaries, and for similar motives. They believed in God's call, and they responded to it in faith. For the kingdom, they sacrificed the joy of having a wife or husband and children of their own to cherish. For God and for service of others they said yes to the laws the Church had made. Volunteers were needed for work in the vineyard, and they enlisted. Besides, they were not alone; and what could be more joyful than to work together in the vineyard of the Lord, digging, pruning, laying sulfate, and in golden October days, reaping the harvest. The new wine dripping from the wine press at the end of the day's labor assails the nostrils and inebriates the heart, and yet this deep joy derived from working in the Lord's vineyard is completely devoid of meaning outside of a life of faith.

These men and women encountered Christ as a friend, or prophet, or master. This is the reason they answered His call. Others responded fearing because of their sins, or because of the dangers of the world, or again through fear of contamination by the flesh. They are all there, called from every human condition, just as when Christ walked the earth, and called this one from his nets, another from his counter or his stall . . . or even from a life of prostitution. They followed because it was Christ who called and because there was work to be done, but all the time the response was made in faith, because Christ is someone to whom one gives one's faith without having seen Him as one sees an ordinary man. I loved Him without ever having met Him in the sense that I can meet a friend or a spouse.

We know also that here and now we already receive a reward. One day Peter said to Jesus: "We have left all things and followed you." Jesus replied: "Truly, I say to you, there is no one who has left house or brothers or sisters or mother or father or children or lands for my sake and for the gospel, who will not receive a hundredfold now in this time, houses and brothers and sisters and mothers and children and lands, with persecutions, and in the age to come eternal life" (Mt. 10:28-30).

Neither Mark nor Matthew expressly mentions the word "wife," but it is understood in the word "house." Luke, however, whose list is shorter, uses the word deliberately. The Lord, who promises the hundredfold even in this world, shows a sense of humor in adding for good measure to the recompense persecutions! But it is in faith alone that the reward is possessed.

Here is to be found the ever contemporary meaning of celibacy chosen for Christ and for the kingdom. How can the disciple ask to be treated otherwise than his master? The final plea of the one who consecrates himself to Christ will be: "Give me your love and that is all I need." Is it not that which seals the love pact between bride and groom? Union takes place beyond the gift. Now this love which ought to be all-sufficing is only grasped in faith. Those who enjoy conjugal intimacy may very well pity us for not knowing what it is to love. But let them be reassured. The love of God, understood in faith, even in a dark manner, is nearer, surer, sweeter, stronger, more consoling, and more intoxicating than any other love. In faith, we are sure with a certainty that no experience can ever give. There lies the meaning of the words of Sacred Scripture: "I will espouse thee in faith" (Hos. 2:20).

Chapter 11

Knowing Love

Those who choose a celibate life ought to know what it is to love and to be loved. To have lived in a family of happy parents, brothers, and sisters where love was given and received; to have known a particular love and to have experienced a thrill of pleasure on hearing news of that person—all this is genuine love. It is also genuine love to have had intimate friends and to have feared for them in time of trouble. For those who have enjoyed love or deep friendship of this kind, God has little difficulty in manifesting Himself. He can also stretch out His hand and touch the heart, just as when—in the lovely image of Michelangelo—He stretched out His hand and gave life to Adam. It is not required of a candidate for celibacy that he first experience the depths of love for someone of the opposite sex, but it is good that he know something of its first stirrings.

For some boys and girls, God is their great friend. Some of them discover, later on, that this attraction toward Christ was a mere childish love affair; but for others again, this was not the case. These latter can truly say that very early in life they gave Him their heart and never went back on that gift. Love of Jesus increased and deepened as their knowledge of Him matured just as the love one bears toward a friend or a fiancé grows as one comes to know him or her more intimately

... until the day when each looked into the eyes of the other, as lovers do, and the bond was sealed forever.

These are realities one cannot ignore. The eye of a child is purer than that of the adult, and the mystery of the gospel message is very real for him. And that is why the great love of a lifetime is able to take root at an early age. As the child matures into adolescence and adulthood, Christ reveals Himself anew. It can often happen that the unloved child finds in Jesus a true friend. In this case, it is Christ alone who awakens in the child's heart a love which goes beyond every other love.

Love of this kind can disappear at the moment of adolescence, when a boy or girl becomes aware of the possibility of other loves; but after a certain eclipse, while the heart seeks to acquire other dimensions, it can also return stronger than before. If, however, the boy or girl has—even if only for an instant—known the happiness of loving and of being loved, should God then choose to call them to a life of celibacy, the suffering experienced can be very keen indeed.

This love of Christ is not at all an abstract thing, but grows like any other love. A spiritual relationship is established with Christ, a relationship which can only develop within celibacy. Christ reveals Himself in the gospel. He lives and speaks under the very eyes of him or her whom He chooses to draw to Himself and to His love. At times this love manifests itself in admiration without limits. At other times, the heart is captivated all of a sudden. However, this is not the moment to enter into the details of such an experience. Let us simply recognize that it is often—I don't say always—in such experiences that the seeds of a vocation to celibate love take root in the heart.

If, for one reason or another, the boy or girl in question finally marries, the marriage will have a new dimension, for it is impossible to have in this way tasted divine love without being at the same time enriched in one's human loving. The experience of divine love is not going to make either party prudish or timid—far from it—for only God's love can lend total transparency to the expression of human love in the flesh.

There is an experience not directly attached to the Person of Jesus in the gospel: that of a divine love which embraces us, penetrates our inmost being, and completely fills us, by communicating its life to us. If we look into the depths of our being, we can grasp with our minds the act that gave us life, as well as the love of our parents. If we descend farther into the depths, we find ourselves face to face with God who created us out of love. We thus encounter love, a love to which, perhaps, we cannot respond except by renouncing marriage.

This love is evident throughout creation. The joy of discovery plunges us more deeply into the life that animates everything and before which we are mute with admiration. But it can also happen that God Himself, independently of His creation, holds us in suspense, alone and before His face. At such a moment, rather than draw life from the rivers which water the plains, we go right to the source, just as the Indian ascetic goes to the mouth of the Ganges. Man can drink at this divine source with a companion, but often he who has heard the call from the fountainhead can only go there unaccompanied. Who could be his companion when he plunges himself in the waters of that love which creates him and sustains him in being?

Later on, when the source has effected his purification, and strengthened him with a new vigor, he can retrace his steps, and in his inner solitude invite his friends to plunge with him into a love which is the origin of all love. "Lord, you have captivated my heart, and I can find no words to sing your praises. It is you who have left me wordless, and there is no one with whom I can communicate. You have drawn me so far away that there is nobody I can invite to accompany me. I shall journey alone then, utterly alone, but I know that when my solitude is perfect, all men will come together in my heart to drink in company with me at the fountain of all love."

Chapter 12

To Whom Shall
I Compare Thee?

We can only love that which is good and true and beautiful. Now theologians tell us that God is all this, but they express themselves in terms so academic that their language is difficult to understand. And yet we know that God has power to win the hearts of those to whom He reveals Himself. The face of the man who has gazed on God is radiant. But it is not enough that God be beautiful. He must also inspire the heart to love, otherwise we should hardly feel attracted to Him; otherwise we could neither love Him nor choose Him in preference to a creature.

No one to my mind has better expressed why he loved God than the great St. Augustine, that ardent lover of beauty. After long searchings, which he describes in his *Confessions,* he discovered God, and in the same work he reveals what he loves when he loves his God:

> "But, what do I love, when I love Thee? Not the prettiness of a body, not the gracefulness of temporal rhythm, not the brightness of light (that friend of these eyes), not the sweet melodies of songs in every style, not the fragrance of flowers and ointments and spices, not manna

and honey, not limbs which can be grasped in fleshly embraces—these I do not love, when I love my God. Yet I do love something like a light, a voice, an odor, food, an embrace, when I love my God—the light, voice, odor, food, embrace of my inner man, wherein for my soul a light shines, and place does not encompass it, where there is a sound which time does not sweep away, where there is a fragrance which the breeze does not disperse, where there is a flavor which eating does not diminish, and where there is a clinging which satiety does not disentwine. This is what I love when I love my God" (*Confessions,* Bk. X, Chap. 6).

St. Augustine was well aware that he could never love anything outside of beauty, but a beauty that had the power to touch the very marrow of his being. Even though God be completely other, He can only win us by touching our hearts, just as does every other love. This divine touch moves us, and makes the heart tremble like the touch of human love, but it touches us so deeply that its quality is perceived as divine.

When two persons love each other truly, they know, see, and feel themselves interior one to the other in a way that has nothing in common with carnal union. No matter how deeply I descend into my being, I find the other; in this other who is completely interior to my "self" I find myself; and in this new self, there again I find the other intimately present. Thus it is, as long as two human beings go on discovering each other in the depths of their consciousness. But it is good at times that they halt for a moment in this mutual search for the other in order to contemplate in silence the depths of their dual mystery.

But God extends His invitation still further, inviting us to penetrate into interior solitudes, vaster and deeper than before. To what shall I compare this love that is being offered to me? Divine love has no comparison outside itself, yet in human love we have a wonderful symbol.

Before knowing what it is to love someone of the opposite

sex, a boy or a girl may experience divine love so deeply that it eclipses all further love experiences. They may discover human love later on and taste its joys, but if their first experience was of the kind I have described above, they will soon realize that no matter how deep the experience of human love, it can never take hold of one's being in as intimate a manner as can a love that is divine. Human love, however, linked as it is to the pleasure and to the ecstasy of the whole being, can call into question the reality of divine love. A virginal love of Christ can even cede its place to sexual love. Conversely, however, this former love can triumph, and forever, over all the affection.

Therein lies its glory. Normally this love of Christ enters by a secret door that man finds only with difficulty. It surges up from the depths of his being with the life it communicates. As with all love, its discovery is slow. It can have its difficult moments, doubts which long conversations are powerless to dispel, sufferings, too, which linger on in spite of tender caresses.

Love can only blossom when confidence and faith have prepared the way. Perhaps for a long time the road lies open, but the door remains closed. Every love entails long moments of waiting. No one should complain about that. In the end, divine love reveals itself. How many married people, too, long for that intimacy and for that union which Christ grants to those whom He loves.

Chapter 13

The Deep Wound

It is not without suffering that one remains celibate for the Lord and His kingdom. Union of heart and mind, indeed of one's very life with God and the Church, is no guarantee that one will not feel deeply the sacrifice of the love of a husband or wife and of children born of that love. It is all very well to sing of God's love, of espousals with the community, of the gift of self to one's fellow man. The desire to love, not in obscurity of faith, but in the bliss of an embrace, will assail us when perhaps we least expect it.

The sight of happily married people, radiating their mutual love, may very well enkindle anew in our hearts the longing for human affection; and there is absolutely no reason to worry if this happens. It is simply a sign that we are normal human beings. Let us rather rejoice at others' happiness, but without seeking to enjoy what we have given up, and without allowing our imagination to dwell on what it would be like to have a dearly-loved wife or a beloved husband. This emotion welled up in our hearts as the sap wells up from the earth in springtime, because such emotion is natural to every human being. But we need harbor no regrets, entertain no jealousies, even if the longing to find ourselves in the arms of someone we love dearly is at times imperious.

Celibacy is not a sort of third sex which is neither male nor female. It does not destroy what is deepest in us, and it is only natural that the desire to act according to our sexual nature sometimes manifests itself. Since we have vowed our virginity to God, there are certian joys which for us are out of bounds; and yet in our imagination and in our dreams we may experience the desire for them, without really intending to do so. That should not unduly worry us. On the contrary, it should contribute to our human maturation in the celibate life we have dedicated to God.

This experience of which I speak, and which is nothing other than the desire for sexual pleasure and conjugal intimacy, has also the effect of making us understand more clearly the meaning of chastity within celibacy. To be chaste when one is celibate is not to have killed the sexual instinct and so to have become in a sense super-human. Rather it is to refrain from yielding to its attraction or from seeking it or from dwelling on it with complacency. And the reason? Because our love is elsewhere. A person may be completely overwhelmed by carnal longings welling up in his heart despite himself, and yet at the same time perfectly free in their regard. In such an experience, the love we have consecrated to God shines like a pearl in troubled waters, or blossoms as does the lotus flower in a muddy pond. Chastity is a lantern for the spirit and a light for the heart. It can flower radiantly in flesh that is tormented.

Thus it happens that a person can experience at one and the same time, the strongest carnal desires and a love of God that is astonishingly pure. Beyond the clamor of sensuality, the heart is strangely peaceful; for the will is firmly established in Him whose love it has chosen.

However, it may happen that the feelings demand satisfaction, and that the longing to satisfy the sexual instinct overpowers the will. At first the will resists the battering, but finally under reiterated blows capitulates, not knowing quite how to defend itself. It had been fascinated at first, then seduced, until finally it gave in when at the beginning it could just as well have turned aside. However, it is extremely difficult to pass judgment in such a case. Each one must be perfectly honest with himself and not try to delude himself with facile excuses. In many cases it is as if the will were ravished. The assaults are so violent that it ultimately yields—and very often not in view of the pleasure it will derive from yielding, but simply to end the struggle and have peace. Some prefer in such cases to acknowledge that they have sinned, desired pleasure, sought it even, when in actual fact there was all the time, deep down, a strong driving force which said no.

Such is the paradox of our existence; we are never as completely master of our acts as we should like to be. An experience of this nature usually leaves in its wake a deep sense of guilt, while in fact it should simply give a clearer picture of the reality. He who esteems his chastity highly must live and relive the sad experience of his helplessness, and realize that chastity is in the spirit, not in the flesh. If we look deeply into our heart, we shall see that even when drawn in spite of ourselves into the experience of sexual pleasure, the heart can remain more faithful than ever to Christ. If it were not so, it would not suffer so intensely at the thought of being unfaithful.

Chapter 14

Necessary Restraints

It is an all too common error to confuse personal fulfillment with liberty to do as one pleases. Many think that they cannot fulfill themseves if there is the slightest obstacle put in their way. When they talk about development according to their deepest tendencies, what they really claim is the ability to do just as they please.

Every art has its restraints. If the art of arts is to have transcended these restraints, it is no less true that each art has had to pass through the same school, and be subjected to a certain number of restrictions, until it mastered them, dominated them, and finally surpassed them in order to attain perfect liberty. This liberty, then, acquired by someone who has mastered these restraints, is capable of achieving great things. Every other kind of liberty is doomed to produce mere jellyfish.

Love, too needs restraints so that it may grow into a love that is real. The superficial kind, purely physical, burns itself out in childish ecstasy, but never can it discover the word or gesture, the attitude or the glance that expresses total giving. As long as love remains at the level of technique, one can say with truth that a relationship has been established, but that is not love. There is an art belonging to an entirely different order than all the techniques one can employ in order to awaken desire and pleasure in the other. Now this art is everything that encourages love to dig its roots deeper and deeper until it becomes a genuine love of person for person.

All human love must be ready for restrictions and even to say no to certain things. It cannot shake off every restraint, for the simple reason that it is an encounter between two persons and two liberties. It is accompanied by a tremendous respect for the other, and a constant attention, which demands renunciation of one's own ideas and of one's own feelings. Every love must likewise guard itself against attractions which might disturb its peace or cause it to deviate toward another person. Love which is at the heart of celibacy can only grow if it keeps a constant watch on its purity. There must be no flirting according to one's whims under the pretext that it is just innocent fun. Love is not something to play around with. In order that it truly grow in us, it must be uncompromising. However pleasant or perhaps even innocent it may be to entertain an affection which in any way troubles the heart, it must be given up once it is perceived that it hampers the freedom of our gift to God. One must experience—even unto tears—that God is our sole lover.

Every relationship, then, which means a division of the heart consecrated to God must be given up. Only an affection capable of being wholly integrated into the love we have given to God can be entertained. This is a fundamental principle not alone of celibate, but also of married love.

If, as it sometimes happens, one takes back some of the love offered to God because He seems so far away and the heart craves for human affection, this lapse through weakness should be the exception, and one should fight to the bitter end in order to remain faithful to the unique love.

Every man knows that, if he allows himself too much liberty with a woman, he risks getting caught in the net once she senses that she is loved and sought after. The same may be said of the woman who plays with a man's feelings. Those who remain celibate for the kingdom are often surprisingly naive in such matters. Perhaps they think they already enjoy angelic privileges. Their affectivity has not gone through the normal maturation process, and they do not seem to have experienced how vulnerable they are in this regard.

However this necessary prudence should express itself neither in coldness nor in fear of the other sex. A man or a woman perfectly conscious of what they are, ought to know how to behave. Awkwardness, coldness, want of simplicity are caused by lack of self-knowledge as well as by one's inability to assess one's own reactions and the reactions one is liable to provoke in others.

Restraint, then, ought to help that liberty which is founded on deep internal peace to grow and expand in us. We know exactly how far to go in our words and in our actions, what we can say to this person or how we can express our affection toward the others. Besides, we know the strength of our will and singleness of our eye. We know that we can hear all without wavering, and yet a declaration of love or affection has power to move us. If we are sure of ourselves, we can receive and even welcome affection and make it our own, rejoice at it and allow it to penetrate into the recesses of our heart where it will enrich our powers of loving.

If the love of God is not sufficiently strong in us to keep us from stumbling now and again, we must put up defenses here and there, at the danger spots which cause us to lose our balance. But we cannot place defenses everywhere. If a relationship troubles us and we can avoid that person, then it is prudent to see him less often. If that is not possible, then we must turn more frequently toward the Lord, in such wise that the human attraction becomes oriented toward the Lord and thus loses some of its *brilliance* in the light of the divinity.

Chapter 15

Freedom of the Spirit in the Flesh

Love of husband and wife grows within and beyond its sexual expression. During the period of engagement, this love was already marvelously fulfilled before the encounter in the flesh. And now in marriage, in the transparency of bodies and beyond the mutual embrace, it must find its ultimate meaning. Thus love becomes free according as it liberates itself from the domination of the flesh, not in order to deny the latter or lay it aside, but to inspire it and to give it its full symbolic value: that of presence.

The celibate must acquire such control of his body, such mastery of his reactions, looks, and imagination that he can enter into a personal, intimate relationship with all those who have need of help or company or affection. Many people seek help from priests or Sisters. What they ask for is advice, but what they are looking for above all is a little sympathy and affection. Those who receive such confidences must be able freely to give of their time and attention and, if necessary, of their friendship or their love, to which every human being has a right to aspire. There are far too many people among those consecrated to God, whose influence is almost nil because they are incapable of human relationships of the kind I have just described. Celibacy has weaned them to such an extent from all affection that they have forgotten how to love. In their closed world, they live like old bachelors or spinsters, and those who come looking for a little attention or affection are regarded as intruders who either annoy them or scare them away.

This is perhaps an exaggeration, but far too often there is little if any human warmth in such relationships. And I don't mean by this that we must throw our arms around all who come to see us. That might be mere comedy, or a kind of philanthropy, instead of love of God. This is not what Christ asks of us when he commands us to love one another. It is true that Christ's love was universal, but, as the gospel clearly shows us, He did not distribute His affection in neat packets prepared in advance. His relationships, on the contrary, were always intensely personal. He did not, for example, say to Martha and to Mary: "Sit down there, both of you, and listen to me, and take care! No jealousy." Martha was loved as much as Mary was, but in another way. Besides, her complaint was not that she was loved less, but that all the work was left to her. She, too, would have liked to have been completely free to listen to Jesus; yet I'm not so sure, because I think she must have been happy to prepare a meal for Him whom she loved.

The whole idea is to attain perfect liberty in our human relationships, so that in all truth we can tell people that we love them for themselves as they are, and not just their "souls"; that our love is real and not simply "for the love of God," as we used to say. We must, then, be able to manifest—and without the slightest ambiguity—perfect controlled human affection. As this mastery is more difficult to acquire when one is young, it is wise, very wise, to discipline oneself severely in this matter and over a long period if one wishes to arrive at perfect friendship in the celibate state.

There is always the possibility here of self-deception, i.e., deluding ourselves that we have arrived at perfect freedom in regard to the flesh. Now this freedom can only grow in the light of our knowledge of the human heart. The pure have the single eye, but it is not the naive purity of childhood, but the purity of an adult who has measured, gauged and explored every crevice of his personality.

As I happen to be speaking about liberty with regard to the flesh, let me say a word here about the liberty which certain persons claim and which is in reality a false interpretation of the phrase "To the pure all is pure." These people think that they have achieved such freedom with regard to their feelings and their bodies in general that they are now free to hold hands, to caress and embrace each other, and all this under the pretext that this is quite a normal way of expressing an affection which is spiritual. This is precisely what the Middle Ages sect, the "Cathares," or "the pure," as their name signifies, claimed. They were so-called because they believed themselves completely free from carnal assaults. We can guess the normal consequences of such theories. The flesh very soon makes its demands. For a time, it appears to have been quenched by the power of the spirit, but all of a sudden it reasserts itself, dragging the spirit with it to its own proper satisfaction. I am fully aware that nothing can better be compared to the deep joy of the spirit than the joy one experiences in loving someone dearly. But when a person has vowed his virginity to God, it is a foolish mistake to walk again along the road which leads to conjugal love.

Chapter 16

Solitude and the Lonely Heart

Those who have renounced marriage experience very keenly the pain of solitude, not only physical solitude, but, more keenly still, solitude of heart. This feeling can be joined to a deep union with God. In fact, solitude is necessary for the growth of celibacy that is of the love of Christ and of men.

This solitude can often manifest itself very early in the life of young priests, religious and consecrated lay people. It can be painful because constant. Every day I see young couples, men and women, pass me by, women carrying their babies, young lovers, married people who have arrived at maturity. Each one goes his way, and it seems to me that solitude is unknown to them. In the evening when I am alone, these images haunt my imagination. In vain I try to think of God and to realize that He is in my heart ... my loneliness remains.

One must learn to live with, indeed desire this solitude, because it is essential to the growth of love consecrated to God. Many fear it, just as many pause in their journey at the edge of the desert, when they ought to go right ahead into its wilderness in order to find God there. There is no need to go in search of the dark night described by St. John of the Cross.

Daily life lived in the state of consecrated celibacy is a wonderful road of contemplation and of union, in a desert solitude.

When this loneliness overpowers us, then is the moment to turn toward God and to say to Him again that we want to answer His call and we must trust and go on trusting in His love, reminding ourselves that He is nearer to us than the most loving of spouses or the most faithful of friends. And after all, we must be realistic and admit that often the keenest suffering for married people is precisely their solitude. Alas, it is all too often a solitude without hope of cure. Instead of making an effort to deepen their intimacy, husband and wife accept all too easily this state of affairs as inevitable.

This feeling of solitude ought not to close the heart, but rather to open it up. Loneliness of heart must be taken in hand, understood for what it is, and accepted; and the heart itself must be emptied of every attachment and of all self-seeking. Thus we shall arrive at a state which is one of total presence before God and men, for there is no total presence outside of the experience of solitude.

The image of the empty is a very beautiful one if we give it true significance. An empty heart is a heart that is transparent, purified of all caricatures of loving, a heart which is free of all attachment to itself. The empty heart is finally a heart that is open to the entire universe and capable of welcoming all who come from every corner of the globe.

The more the heart is emptied, the closer it resembles the heart of Christ opened by the lance; the more intense, too, is the love it both gives and receives. It is no longer a love consisting of feelings and words, but a gift of one's whole being. At this point, human love encounters divine love, at the stillpoint, at the ineffable center of our life. There is no language to describe such an experience which leaves one completely silent and which can only be understood by those who share it.

In the case of certain people, this solitude is an unwelcome guest whose company is resented; the result is a heart incapable of loving, hardened and contracted and ultimately closed. God's love has difficulty in expressing itself in such a heart, while those who really grasp the meaning of the desert, love it passionately. There they find God, a God at times "absent," but at the same time ever-present and ever-loving. Such a heart cannot fail to be completely fulfilled, while at the same time completely open to God and to men.

If, normally, God imposes on those whom He has elected long years of human solitude, it is because He wishes to be the sole object of their love. He can literally bar the way to the most legitimate human loves, in order to force us to immerse ourselves all the more deeply in the experience of His unique love. In any case, it is wise to remember that it is only after many years of absolute fidelity to celibacy for the love of our Lord that we can arrive at the kind of friendship we are now going to talk about.

Chapter 17

Friendship and Love

The rediscovery of friendship and love within celibacy is one of the most important facts of the spiritual history of our times. This rediscovery goes hand in hand with the defection of thousands of persons who believed that the only way to solve their problem was to abandon the celibacy they had originally assumed. I have no intention here of questioning the difficulties which led so many people to abandon their vocation. I am convinced, however, that if such persons had been aware of the extraordinary possibilities of friendship, of intimacy, indeed of love, which a perfectly lived celibate life offers, they would not have so easily sought in marriage a remedy for their problems.

Many consecrated persons still think that, for them, a friendship which is in any way a deep relationship is a blemish on their vow of celibacy. It seems to them that once the heart is given to God, it is closed forever to all love outside of Him. They fear attachments, the joys of proffered friendships, the normal unambiguous expressions of affection. There are in the world mountains of love, oceans of sympathy, which have neither donor nor receiver. Surely those whose business it is to bear witness to God's love should be the first to give and to receive that love. Let them sow around them seeds of joy and sympathy; let them also reap the harvest springing forth from the hearts of men who know that they are sincerely loved.

Friendship in celibacy opens up a marvelous world which

develops far beyond the erotic, the carnal, or the sentimental. On the contrary, one discovers what it means to love someone for what he is in himself, in other words, as Christ loves him. This love is entirely human, though not expressed sexually, as it is in marriage, and for which such expression is reserved. Such friendship and such love admit one into the mystery of human intimacy, offered to those who have renounced marriage for the Lord and for His kingdom.

Can the one who has said to Christ, "I give my heart to you alone," allow a friendship which may be as deep as the greatest love to grow in his heart? Immediately there rises before him the spectre of what one used to call "particular friendships" and also of what now has come to be known as "the third way." What one objects to—and rightly so—in "particular friendships" is the fact that they are particular and exclusive, linking together, as they do, two persons in an affection which annoys everybody and at the same time prevents them from maturing within the circle of their own community. Such particular friendships are adolescent in character. They must be pruned and transformed into the open kind, without any exclusiveness and without any trace of ambiguity. As for the "third way," which would allow celibates to enjoy intimacies and tender caresses which belong uniquely to the married state, such behavior can only be justified by lying to oneself.

Deprived as they are of the help of a partner, consecrated persons often feel keenly the need for human support. After all, God is God, and at times seems very far away. The friend may be one's spiritual director, or a fellow worker, or one whom one meets frequently. He may also be one to whom one is linked by an indescribable affinity, by a compatibility so deep that neither distance nor absence can affect it; and even after years of separation this compatibility is felt because it is always present. Whether in one's company or far away, the friend is a treasure. And God desires that those who have given their lives to Him may, if necessary, find someone, man or woman, who will give to His invisible love a human face, to His unspeakable tenderness a human expression.

Chapter 18

Wonderful Intimacy

In friendships between persons of the same sex, the possible dangers are exclusiveness and excessive sentimentality. However, such tendencies can be kept in perfect control if one does not allow oneself to be blinded to the realities of human nature. Thus can develop a deep friendship contributing in no small way to human and spiritual development, for nothing can better help us to love God than to know that we are capable of loving and of being loved.

The real difficulty begins, however, when the friendship is with a person of the opposite sex. It is not reasonable to give a systematic denial to every friendship of this kind; neither is it wise to enter lightly into such a relationship. Great prudence is necessary, for what began by being a spiritual friendship has very often ended carnally. Besides, it is not by surrounding a friendship whose motive is unavowedly sensual with spiritual trappings that one avoids misfortune. Every friendship which is idealistic and which idealizes the beloved has already begun to deviate. Friendship must be established in the truth.

If, then, the risks are so great in the case of a friendship with a person of the opposite sex, why not cut it out on principle? But we have before us the example of Christ, who blessed friendship and whose friends were men and women. History records few such friendships, but in genuine history, i.e., that written by the lives of men, those who were God's friends and who also enjoyed deep friendship with a fellow man or woman, were very numerous and still are. However, these deep relationships are lived in the depths, and are all the more hidden in the measure that the desires of the flesh have been dominated. They have no reason to be ashamed. They do not conceal their friendship, and yet this intimacy is interior in those hidden depths where God manifests to each His love.

Here we see celibacy producing wonderful results in the natural order. Some of God's friends renounced married love in order to find Him and serve Him, and suddenly one day along the road they met a companion. One or the other was in need of help because of fatigue or worry or doubts or simply because of the long road ahead, and help was asked for and received. Usually both go their separate ways afterwards without ever really having met each other. In other cases, meetings become more frequent and conversations become more and more intimate. Each one is reassured about the sincerity both of the other's gift to God and of his friendship, until one day they realize that their experiences are mutual and that their lives are closely intertwined.

In such a relationship there is no need to fear, except with the prudent fear of one who recognizes his sinful state. Slowly there is created between both persons an indescribable bond in which the flesh has no part, and yet a bond which, while being spiritual, is no less completely human. One is a man; the other, a woman. Of this fact, each is entirely conscious, but beyond the carnal plane. In fact, it is not in their flesh or in their bodily sexuality that men and women are most deeply male and female. It is in their feelings, in their psychology, and in the depths of their personality that a man is a man and a woman a woman. Thus, without knowing themselves man and woman in the flesh, each is aware of the other's sexuality in his total being. It is at this level, also, that husband and wife seek to know and love each other. The two roads, one leading to marriage and the other to celibacy, seem to lead in opposite directions, but in reality they can converge at the limits of human experience. Having reached this degree of intimacy, friends have the feeling of being emptied of self and entirely open to the other person, in such wise that there is effected a kind of mutual indwelling. When each looks into his own heart, there he finds the other; and in his friend he discovers himself in a new form. Thus, in reciprocal interiority, which has neither end nor limit, each discovers the other.

The touchstone of the quality of a union of this kind is this: the deeper it becomes, the more God manifests Himself. The rendezvous such friends assign to themselves, the place where they "touch" each other, is the very place where God meets "and touches" them. While a dubious friendship disturbs the soul and impinges on the unique love, this latter kind is in perfect harmony with the love vowed to God. There are no longer two loves, but one.

It is true that friendships of this kind are rare, but they are not impossible. They must not be attempted unless the object of one's choice is capable of being this perfect friend. It is necessary to wait, to ask a sign of God and to seek His love and it alone, for this friendship demands great self control and a deep sense of the absolute quality of our gift to God. Except for extraordinary cases, it is only after years of detachment and even of sacrifice of the joys of other friendships, that such a friendship can be realized. Experience has proved the truth of this.

Chapter 19

A Heart of Flesh

What we are really asking God to do when we pray Him to remove our hearts of stone and give us hearts of flesh, is to love as He loves us in His Son, with a human heart, that is, with a heart that is sensitive and, above all, capable of suffering.

If the ideal of celibacy is insensibility, then it is no longer Christian. What makes the way of celibacy so difficult is that the celibate heart must remain open and capable of loving without ambiguity. There are many who set out on the road of friendship already described, but who through lack of interior purification fall into the trap of forming relationships that are dangerous, bringing as they do nothing but disappointment in their train and running—as such "friendships" inevitably do—into an impasse. He who at all costs must find the kindred soul runs the risk of making a foolish choice. How many have fallen victims to this error! The danger lies in the subtle search for sexual satisfaction, under the guise of piety.

The beautiful friendships I spoke about cannot—for obvious reasons—reach perfection after only one or two encounters. Some people take refuge in the truism that one cannot be perfect all at once, in order to justify acts and gestures which prudence dictates they should avoid. To allow, at the beginning of a relationship, liberties which belong rather to engaged couples, can prevent a friendship from developing as it ought

to. It it not at this stage a matter to be treated lightly, for the
flesh becomes attached to certain practices more easily and
more quickly than it becomes detached from them.

In a friendship that is too sentimental such desires must immediately be controlled. Finally, the relationship between this
man and this woman should transcend the need which often expresses itself thus: "I need you for my personal fulfillment."
Then a woman will not have to undergo the humiliation of hearing a priest tell her that he needs her in order to be completely
himself. No, she will have truly become his equal, and will no
longer feel she is a mere instrument . . . and indeed at times a
plaything for man.

What one must seek, then, is to free oneself from the sense
of need, so that friendship can grow and develop in the complete liberty of each with regard to the other. It is only normal that the flesh be tormented at times, but one should avoid
pausing to analyze the temptation; above all, one should not
yield to it. All desire of possession, domination, or total abandon should disappear. In the friendship of which there is
question here, man and woman are established in total equal-
ity. They can communicate in absolute lucidity and without
fear or hesitation, thus realizing a union which defies cate-
gory, but whose ideal is the union which Christ brings about
with those whom He loves.

This kind of union is effected in the deepest part of the personality, where God unites Himself to us. That is why friends
find God in this intimate center where there is no obstacle
placed in the way of divine love. This union appears as the
most detached and purest of friendships, veritable love that
it is, a love which can only be realized in perfect chastity.

We may call this union spiritual or mystical marriage, but
here there is danger of falsifying perspectives. Marriage always
carries with it the notion of exclusivity, since sexual union can
only realize itself fully in a unique relationship. The intimacy
which grows within the celibate state cannot be exclusive, since
perfect virginity allows of intimacy with several persons. A
priest, for instance, may be intimate—in the sense we described

above—with several women, who in their turn may have deep relationships with other men.

Now all this is possible only if those who enjoy this network of relationships are free from all sensuality and from every selfish attachment. Such relationships, open to God and to others, cannot achieve their perfection without first passing through darkness, fire, and desert! The way which leads there is painful and tedious, and it is the road which Christ trod. It may take several years before such a friendship can openly declare itself—without risk of deviating. It is ordinary human and spiritual wisdom to acknowledge that, while admitting the wonderful possibilities of deep friendship for those leading a celibate life, we must also state and restate that the road leading thereto may at the same time be a long and arduous one.

When a person thus realizes his vow of celibacy in a setting which allows his whole being to develop, he will be surprised at how far he has traveled along the road. At the beginning of the journey he offered his heart to God with a promise to love no one but Him, and now God gives him back his heart, but this time, a new heart, made of flesh, capable of loving Him and, furthermore, of loving all men. In the faces of his best friends, the celibate sees the face of Christ; and his own face reflects the invisible face of his God.

Chapter 20

Journeyings

The liberty of heart and mind vis-à-vis the flesh which perfect celibacy demands cannot be acquired in the space of a day. Perfect celibacy is, in fact, a very special integration of our faculties of doing, knowing, and loving into a life oriented by faith.

At the moment of choice, the road to take lies clear ahead, for the choice is usually made in great lucidity. But little by little the light seems to grow dim. It may be a trial permitted by God to deepen the faith in the one consecrated to Him; or it may be the result of repeated negligence. The heart becomes less transparent; the spirit darkens; and finally the will flounders. The struggle to prevent anything coming between the heart and God must be kept up to the very end.

The moment those around see me in difficulty they say: "But why not do as everybody else is doing, and get married?" Now this is the very kind of advice that makes perseverance difficult for many, and they finally become convinced that they were victims of an illusion when they thought themselves called to a celibate life.

Soon everything seems to militate against the choice made in faith. Human realities loom large in perspective. Carnal longings and affective yearnings assail the one who has vowed his virginity to God. For some, it is the constant torturing of the flesh itself, the desire to see, to touch, to embrace. For others, it is the need of company, of a loving presence to which one can respond by a total presence. For others again, it may be the longing to be understood, to live intimately in the heart of the other, and to feel the other's presence in one's own. At the same time, the love of Christ reveals itself under different aspects, sometimes as an intimacy so deep and strong and warm, and at the same time so obvious, that the longings just described seem insipid when compared to it. But at other times, this love of Christ is perceived only in faith; and it is then that the heart suffers keenly. Yet it is precisely there that real love takes root. It takes years and years of fidelity in sunshine and rain, in joy and in sorrow, before celibacy becomes the center of our personality, like a diamond heart in a body made of flesh. It takes time, a long time, for this to be effected.

In this domain, one has to be ruthless and uncompromising. Unfortunately, some remain "substantially" faithful only because they allow themselves compensations in the affective and at times in the sensual order. Such practice makes celibacy all the more difficult because it evades navigation in the center of the current.

Being ruthless in one's attitude, however, does not mean that one will not be tempted, or that one will not fall through human weakness, or again that one is not going to look for compensations at the moment of trial when everything goes wrong and one feels the need to love and be loved. But these lapses will not be an obstacle to the onward march of him who, in spite of weaknesses, rests firm in his resolve.

We must be very clear about this question of love and friendship for celibates. The friendship described in these pages may appear too lofty, too idealistic, even inhuman; and yet experience proves that it is, on the contrary, realistic. Thus, we must look at it as an ideal which is possible of attainment. To avoid all misunderstanding, it is necessary to repeat here that in the early years of priestly or religious life one must deliberately say no to certain friendships which cannot be lived with perfect freedom for the simple reason that the affective or the sensual elements are still too captivating.

And yet, young people can experience friendships that are very pure. Such friendships are a wonderful safeguard to chastity, giving it light, force, and inspiration, and yet here again one must not be presumptuous.

A friendship which has thus grown in the light of faith, and in an effort to be constantly more faithful, can flower perfectly when the integration of all its aspects has been accomplished. Such is the law of human life. It takes time for virginity to take possession of our entire being, opening it up both to God and men, but we know that time spent in the service of faith works wonders.

Part Three

Celibacy for Our Times

Chapter 21

A Light for Our Times

In presenting Himself and His disciples as eunuchs, Christ certainly intended the impact to be as great as when He proclaimed, "Blessed are the poor," yet at the present time it is Christian poverty that appears particularly attractive. History has ordained it so. Now is the ideal moment to bear witness to poverty, in a world so harassed by misery and suffering; and if there is in our day a great deal of discussion about the Church of the poor, it is because of the desire to single out from Christ's teaching a capital point for modern times.

Now is not the witness of celibacy also something which our times desperately need? Does not the modern world also need this friendship, this gift of oneself, about which I spoke and which is a fruit of celibacy? Is not that also a light which can shine in the darkness?

Not very long ago, surveys were made in mission countries to ascertain how celibacy was viewed there. In certain places, for example in Thailand, where there are thousands of Buddhist monks, the reply was that it was held in high esteem. This esteem can, however, be allied with a certain disdain, for celibates come to be regarded as lazy people and the parasites of society. In the majority of cultures, religious celibacy is practically unheard of, with the result that many draw the conclusion that it has no meaning in these countries and that the Church should, without further delay, ordain married men to the priesthood. This argument, however, is a shortsighted one. Christ never made a sociological survey to determine how He ought to present the ideal of the perfect disciple. Rather His notion of the "priesthood" was revolutionary! Christ's own priesthood was not an institutional one, and we may well ask the question: what would He think of a purely functional priesthood?

Let us admit it: celibacy is not understood in our day, but was it any better understood in Christ's time? Yet He proposed it as an ideal, knowing perfectly well that only those to whom the Father revealed it could understand. It is in this sense that celibacy, more explicitly than marriage, witnesses to faith in God. In presenting it as He did, Christ opened the way to a new relationship with His Father, a way which bears witness to God's absolute being in a more radical way than does marriage. Such a road to sanctity does not make him who answers God's call more perfect than married people, but God has need of persons who will bear testimony to the fact that He is the source of all love, and that in Him is realized every other possibility of loving.

I am also of the opinion that celibacy, truly lived, can be a wonderful beacon at times when all barriers are down, when pleasure is for the asking, when the current idea is that everything is permissible. And all this with the object, it is claimed, of freeing love from false inhibitions. But is it true that the ability to make love at a whim strengthens and deepens love? The very opposite is the case. The more one plays about with love, the less likely one is to find it.

One of the characteristics of our modern civilization is that we exist at skin-level, and the subtle researches carried out by psychologists cannot alter that fact. We live at the surface of things and at the same time aspire desperately after a life lived in depth. No one can deny that it is the presence within Christianity of thousands and thousands of true celibates that has brought about a deepening of conjugal love, for there is always the danger that human love will stagnate if it ceases for a moment to plunge further and further into deep waters.

Eunuchs for the kingdom of heaven are constant reminders

that beyond what we normally call "love" is to be found love itself. Marriage and virginity are but two aspects of the one reality, each proclaiming in its own way love's marvels. Both roads lead to the same destination: one road is proposed to the vast majority; the other, to a minority whom God calls by a sign. It is by knowing well men and women who seek God either in marriage or through celibacy that one comes to understand why both states are necessary in order to throw light on the mystery of the human person, on human relations, and on our relationship with God.

At a time when the Holy Spirit is manifesting Himself anew in the Church, celibacy will once more become meaningful to our world. It is here, in fact, that the Holy Spirit should find a privileged "field" for His divine activity.

Finally, what does our modern world lack most, if not men and women who are perfectly free, free not only to help by giving their possessions to others, but free in the sense that they are completely docile to the inspiration of the Holy Spirit?

Chapter 22

Celibacy without Barriers

It was in order to render more eloquent the witness borne by celibacy that the barriers protecting it were removed. The result, however, was that many subsequently opted for marriage and are no longer to be found in the ranks of those witnessing to a divine love beyond the normal human condition. Others, while still claiming to be witnesses to consecrated celibacy, come to terms with so many infidelities that it is hard to see what exactly it is they are testifying to. Now this does not make the witness of those who remain truly faithful any easier. Unable to point the finger at any breach of mores, hostile critics of the latter dub them, instead, hypocrites, and so it is easy to understand why many are discouraged in the face of such a situation. But, after all, the Lord did remind us that the world cannot possibly understand certain follies which His love inspires in men's hearts.

In former times, Sisters were enclosed behind a grill because it was held that a woman ought to be protected either by a husband or by the walls of a convent, with the result that the struggle was long and hard before permission could be obtained for them to leave their convents in order to devote themselves to works of charity. But now, barriers are down, convents are open; and many religious no longer wear a distinctive habit. Normally, however, they wear some kind of sign to indicate that they are religious.

The same applies to priests, who in this matter are even freer than are Sisters. In some countries, their preference for certain styles of lay dress results, not in a concern that they be mistaken for laymen, but in the latter's fearing that one day they are going to be addressed as "Father." As one humorist put it: "The one you thought was the parish priest's friend, is the priest." Many priests wear a small cross on the lapel, but that too is tending to disappear. After all, laymen do not wear it!

We have traveled a long way since the time when the wearing of a cassock was of obligation, the stated motive being that it was a safeguard to chastity. In certain mission countries, priests wore a beard for the same reason. However, we must not be ironical toward those who have gone before us, knowing as we do that future generations will have like sentiments in our regard. In the measure that they take their own ideas seriously, they will find reason to laugh at what to them appears as our silly ways.

It is very difficult to know to what degree the removal of barriers, together with the liberty to come and go as one pleases, has contributed to defections. The older regime, outwardly without great problems, often hid great misery. But everything was done to avoid scandal. Things were fixed up quietly behind the scenes, and priests were able to resume their ministry as before. A page had simply been turned over. Now that the Church is more ready to grant dispensations, many priests, as well as religious men and women, easily accept the hypothesis of a relationship which may entail the abandoning of celibacy, thus slipping more easily past the line of no return.

If a priest or a Sister finds that celibacy is too heavy a burden to carry, it is easy for him or her to take advantage of a temptation, or indeed to put themselves directly in its path. Once sense desires are allowed free play, the barriers protecting chastity fall down with little difficulty. And yet, the approach of infidelity is often very subtle. A good person will not be deceived by vulgar attractions. A pious "virtuous" woman will have more power over a priest's heart than will any other kind of woman.

When a priest or a Sister has practically complete liberty to meet whomsoever they will, when and where they will, there are no barriers except those they themselves choose to place. If they have a real love for the Lord, His Church, and the Christian community, they will know very well what to do in order to safeguard their vocation. They must first of all be absolutely determined on loyalty to the engagement entered into with the Lord. It is an engagement of honor, a pact of friendship, an oath of espousal for life. It engages the very depths of one's being, for it is the gift of person to person. God alone knows how many times since Christ walked the earth men and women consecrated to Him have said no to pleasure they could have enjoyed, for the simple reason that deep down in their hearts someone whom nobody could see whispered to them: "I have espoused thee in faith."

As contacts between men and women are now much freer than they used to be, development in the state of celibacy has become easier; and while sexual relations must always be excluded, there are many other possibilities of encounter and exchange which permit men and women to grow in mutual knowledge. If each is sure of his conditional attachment to the Lord, then no other barriers are required beyond those which love inspires in the heart. Thus it is possible to develop within celibacy human relations so deep and so enriching that celibates will have no occasion to envy married people, for they themselves will know what it is to love and to be loved.

Chapter 23

Free Men

The age we live in, which from a technological point of view has accomplished so much, has destroyed that amalgam which is man, by separating one component from the other. Is humanity not paying dearly for technological involvement, in sacrificing to it the noblest element in man's being? And the great loser in the affair is man himself, who no longer knows either who he is or what he is capable of doing, lost as he is in a world of which he is no longer master. The greater and more wonderful the instruments fashioned by man, the more likely he is to become enslaved by them. And he is experiencing in every domain this lack of freedom; on the one hand the press and television indoctrinate him; on the other, advertisers use all their art to entice him this way and that. Society has become more and more complex, and free men are going to be harder and harder to find.

Now he who has vowed his virginity to God can—given a normal personality development in the celibate state—achieve a freedom which will enable him to be at the disposition of all those seeking their identity and a meaning to their lives. I know that at the present time many renounce celibacy in order the better to approach men and their problems. Sometimes, however, they renounce it because they have not been able to attain the freedom of heart which celibacy demands. They had doubts about their mission; and instead of remaining on the bank, like John at the Jordan, so as to point to the Lord hidden in the crowd, they allowed the crowd to take hold of them, and now there is no mystery in their lives to which they can bear witness. In other words, they are no longer free men. They have been freed from a certain number of restrictions, but they have not attained to that true liberty of heart and mind which alone makes one sensitive to the mystery of God and of His creatures.

They renounced celibacy because it was something they were obliged to "preserve," while, in fact, the problem is not that of remaining a virgin, but of becoming one. To "remain" a virgin, to "preserve" one's virginity is nothing more than the renunciation of marriage, of conjugal love, of motherhood or of fatherhood. No personality ever developed by amputation!

No one can become truly celibate without squarely facing every stage of human existence. It is, in fact, impossible to realize fully the ideal of celibacy when one is twenty, at the moment when one makes the decision to give oneself to God. But to say at forty, "I did not know what I was giving up at twenty," is to show that one has already refused the human condition, which is to realize in our mature years what we promised at the age of twenty. To "preserve" one's celibacy is to create it at every moment. When Christ bade us keep His commandments, what He was asking us to do was to fulfill them.

It is here perhaps that our generation shows its greatest weakness, believing as it does that liberty means non-engagement, being at the beck and call of the senses, the slave of the passing moment. Furthermore, young people, claiming to be mature, aspire after maturity for the simple reason that they prefer not to get involved. The world changes at such a rate that projects conceived at the level of human history are constantly being blocked by the turning wheel of existence. This is why too existential a view of human life has given many young people a false idea of freedom, a "freedom" which is ultimately the negation of liberty.

Thanks to the modern sciences, and to the technology which

makes them possible, very long-term projects can be envisaged, while man is no longer capable of making a decision even for his own lifetime!

Now celibate life is perhaps the most perfect opportunity offered to man for the making of a decision which transcends the instability of human life, not by evading that life, but by orienting it toward the ultimate reality of human existence. It is only by leaning on faith in Christ that such a project becomes possible. And in its accomplishment the personality is just as enriched, sometimes even more enriched, than if it had followed the path leading to marriage.

It seems to me that the present era has need of "virgins" of this kind, who testify in a very special way to the presence of God's kingdom even in this world. To be a celibate is to throw into greater relief those aspects of the human person which married life reveals less clearly. To be celibate for Christ and His kingdom is to be a man or a woman in a special kind of way, but in a way which is in every sense as rich as being a man or a woman in the married state.

Chapter 24

The Undivided Heart and the Gift of One's Time

In order to justify priestly celibacy, the reason is often put forward that priests should be able to give all their time to others without a wife or children having to suffer as a consequence. It is easy enough to understand the value of this argument when the priest is, in fact, entirely at the disposition of his flock; but it carries little weight when the priest divides his time, like any business man, between office hours, services of one kind or another, and all the time he wants for going to the movies or watching television. Any sensible person will rightly claim that he might just as well dedicate these leisure hours to a family if he had one. That is why the further one steers toward the idea of a functional priesthood and toward a celibacy conceived only in terms of freedom from family obligations, the less easy it is going to be to require celibacy for the priestly state.

If, however, there is an increasing tendency to reduce the priesthood to a function, its other aspect, that is, total consecration of one's being to God in view of the ministry, must be underlined. I mention the problem again here, simply to restate that a priest ought not to measure his function in terms of hours spent in service, but in terms of interior availability.

His mind and his heart must be perfectly free, so that he can be in truth "for others." Obviously a married priest would be obliged to give a certain amount of his time to his wife and children, making himself thereby less free for his apostolate.

In the great body which is the Church, everything hangs together; and if the Church values celibacy, it is because she wishes her ministers of the word of God to be free both from themselves and for their apostolate. On the other hand, we hear it said repeatedly that, if priests remain unmarried, they are ignorant of many of life's problems; and yet is it not to priests free from family ties and open to all problems that the faithful most readily go to discuss their personal problems?

The reason the Church finally wished to impose celibacy on her priests is that their ministry has to do with man in his entirety. It was her wish that her priests should be free from ties of affection that might be too strong, and so interfere with complete availability and dedication to their mission; that they might be in the world a new revelation of Christ and of His Father's love. In short, it was a total view of the priestly vocation, as an imitation of Christ and as service of His Church, that prompted her to exact of her ministers the renunciation of marriage.

One may say, then, that the Church wished to have priests freed from worldly cares, men "set apart" for the service of God and of the Christian community. In the first place, she wished them to be free from sexual ties; for it was formerly a widespread belief that the sexual act was a mere concession to human frailty, besides being essential to the propagation of the human race.

This "liberation," then, which the Church desired for her priests takes on a different coloring in the light of the religious grandeur of marriage and relations between wife and husband, and requires that it be viewed in a different perspective. However, whatever be the new perspectives with regard to Christian love, celibacy retains its entire value provided it is "completely assumed"; and it cannot be completely assumed unless it is accepted in its entire reality.

Thus we arrive at one of the aspects already alluded to in this problem of celibacy. Marriage is the mutual gift of two persons in a union which binds them heart to heart and flesh to flesh in a unity of mind and affection. No human being can at the same time live two unions of this kind for the simple reason that the harmony depends on habit, on ways of "living with" the other, which engage the body as well as the spirit. Such a union, implying sexual intimacy, demands a one-to-one relationship because at this level it is exclusive. Man can only realize one union at a time, namely, a union which includes at the same time the mind, the heart, and the body in all its sexual reality. Spiritual union, on the contrary, does not require this exclusiveness.

In a relationship not implying a union of bodies, the heart and mind are free to create a greater number of bonds. Married people can also cultivate deep friendships outside the conjugal context, but a totally assumed celibacy, which is at the same time balanced, should be able to allow itself an even greater liberty in this domain. The celibate person's heart is free to love his friends, men and women, with a love neither depending on the flesh nor on the senses, but addressing itself to each person in his undefinable reality.

Chapter 25

Witnesses to God's Love

There is a lot of talk about love; but like all the fundamental realities of life, love cannot be defined. To add to the difficulty, Christ came to tell us that God is love, that we must love one another as He loved us, that is, as He loves His Father and as His Father loves Him. Christ showed us, too, how that love is lived in human life. In Him we find all its dimensions, save the conjugal. "There is no greater love," He says, "than to give one's life for those whom we love." Thus, having shared His life with others during His encounters with them, He communicated it by giving Himself through His death and resurrection in order to be our life forever.

Christ left us no specific teaching about the consecrated life, but He Himself lived in a manner that those who would be inspired to follow Him could imitate. Christ never constrains, nor does He dogmatize in order to clinch a final decision. Instead, He unveils the mystery of God's love. "He who is able to understand, let him understand." This is how all the great spiritual traditions began. In the history of Buddha, we read that one day he picked a flower and, without saying a word, showed it to his disciples. Among those disciples was one who smiled, having understood the mystery, for between him and the Buddha a strange bond had been established. The smile of Buddha's disciple is regarded by Zen adepts as the origin of

their spiritual tradition which requires neither book nor for-
mal teaching in order to communicate itself.

The one who has vowed himself to God ought likewise to be
able to savor beyond all language and all expression the love with
which God loves him and which it is his task to communicate.
But we must remember that it is no abstract, cold, theoretical
love. Those whose privilege it was to meet Christ felt their
hearts burn within them when He spoke to them. While the
Pharisees saw nothing but blasphemy in His words, the crowds
who followed Him—Nicodemus, the Samaritan woman, John,
Andrew, Peter, Martha, Mary, and all the rest—knew that they
were loved by Him, as did the woman taken in adultery whom
everybody condemned.

In the affection which Christ manifested toward His friends,
toward Mary and Joseph, there was an ardor which respected
convention while at the same time going beyond it. One is
shocked perhaps at the terms He employs when referring to
His Mother, and yet the word "woman" carries with it immense dignity and great respect. He calls her "woman" just
as He refers to Himself as "the Son of Man." Like all those
who know what it is to love in truth, Christ was no sentimen-
talist. He enjoys a wonderful liberty in His affections, and the
manner in which He expresses His love for men and women
never shocks or strikes one as unusual.

The priest and the Sister ought to be witnesses of Christ's love.
They ought to be able to give their undivided attention, show
unaffected interest, a solicitude devoid of self-interest, an unambiguous friendship; their love should be neither too tender
nor too passionate, but an affection which leaves the heart free
and does not disturb that of others.

The affection and friendship which they manifest is at the
same time God's and their own. They are not simply inter-
mediaries, messengers of a love outside themselves. On the
contrary, their whole being is engaged in the witnessing of this
love, for who will believe in God's love if he does not find it in
human form, shining on a human face. A priest cannot say
to a woman, "I love you," as an ordinary man might say to a

woman to whom he can show tenderness; but he can say, "God loves you," and in that same movement of love he too loves her. In this sense he can truly say, "I love you"; and such a love can be strong as death, yet it will express itself as the simplest and most unambiguous of friendships. And yet this is not to hide a love behind a friendship. The love of God is a consuming fire which burns our hearts, and yet what love is freer than it from all that is carnal?

But one may ask, how is this possible? We must believe that it is possible since Christ gave us an example and proposes Himself to us as our model. What prevents us from understanding is that we associate, or are made to associate, love with conjugal union, in other words, love and its expression in the flesh. Married persons who live in perfect harmony, physical and otherwise, are the first to tell us that love's expression in the flesh is but a means of increasing a love which goes beyond every embrace, except that interior one which has no way of expressing itself. Why not look on our celibacy as a means of expressing, in our human condition, the love of God which Christ came on earth to reveal, while at the same time we walk hand in hand with so many Christians who realize and manifest that same love in the married state? Thus, the two ways meet, in order to reveal the same love under two different aspects: that of marriage and that of celibacy.

Chapter 26

For the Kingdom

If we vow our life to God in celibacy, it is first and foremost a response to God's love, a response which could not be made in any other way. Such a decision goes beyond human reasoning, and that is why nobody can question its validity, for it defies all human argument. This is its strength as well as its weakness in the eyes of unbelievers. The gift of self to God in celibacy is a response of love to God's love, a personal response to a personal love.

This love is at the same time desired for the kingdom. This can be understood in the sense of a promise on Christ's part that a special place will be reserved to the celibate in His kingdom. But it is, first of all, celibacy for the gospel's sake, for the sake of the good news. Now this good news is not what many today understand it to be, that is, human fulfillment. In order to work in underdeveloped countries it is not necessary that one conform one's life to the lives of those one has come to help.

When everything has been given, when one has got rid of all one's possessions, if one does not know how to love, then there is nothing left to give. Many priests and religious give up the celibate life in order to be closer to the human condition. But what strikes me most in the reasons advanced by them for so doing is the extent to which they are turned in on themselves: personal fulfillment, personal equilibrium, a desire to be like the rest of men. Even if many believe they can better witness to the gospel as married persons, the fact remains that they abandon their state, concentrating all their attention on their own problems. This is probably why the decision they make is so painful. If, on the other hand, these priests and Sisters were more conscious of the kingdom and of their role as Christ's witnesses, they might view celibacy in a more objective way, forgetting themselves for love of others.

In the light of these facts, one is permitted to think that the losers in the celibacy crisis are those who have need of human and spiritual help which only those can give who are completely open, as was Christ, to the divine mystery, and perfectly attentive to the mystery of others. The majority of those who give up the ministry or religious life deprive those who need them so much of a precious aid. Even though lay persons are becoming increasingly more capable of helping one another in the search for God, it remains true that the primary role of the priest or of the Sister is to be a witness to the absolute. Here lies their essential mission. That is what must remain when all the rest has been swept aside.

The Christian world at the present time is hypersensitive about physical poverty, but is it capable of being at the same time sensitive about affective and spiritual poverty? Bread and rice are necessary, true; but so too are understanding and affection. Every human being can devote himself to the task. Those who have discovered love and devotion in marriage can easily devote themselves to others. But what they do points to a charismatic gift of the person himself, a gift which engages man's entire being in his devotion to his fellow man: the breaking of the bread of the spirit and of the heart at the same time as that of the body. Now this charism should be able to develop still more freely in the celibate state. If, however, celibacy closes the heart, it is because it does not find its inspiration either in God's love or in the strength of the Spirit.

In every era, men and women have renounced marriage for some cause or other. How many young girls have given up the idea of having a husband of their own so that they might look after their parents in their old age? Both men and women have sacrificed marriage either for life or for long years, to give themselves to a political cause or to realize a career. There was nothing religious in their motivation. They simply sacrificed personal happiness in order to follow an ideal. Their personality development suffered in no way as a consequence, but the development was effected otherwise than through marriage. Why, then, should those whom the Lord calls to serve Him as celibates, for His love and for the sake of the gospel, consider themselves as outside the race of common men! What makes us appear strange in the eyes of men is that we give up a love that all can see for a love which is invisible. If they cannot see this love which is hidden, let them at least see its fruits in our everyday life.

Chapter 27

As Adults

The present crisis pinpoints how feeble was the motivation toward celibacy in the case of many priests and religious. That it could be abandoned so easily, faith had first to lose its meaning; and in recent years, everything seems to have conspired toward that end. Attention was focused not so much on the realities of the faith as on human realities. Love for one's fellowmen took pride of place, while love of God was quietly relegated to the background. The next step in the chain of logic was the search for a human love, vastly more concrete than love of Christ,

Viewed from the outside, the world of priests and religious gives the impression of a universe of great big children dancing gaily in the sunlight. Their very freedom—itself a gift from on high—seems to have prevented them from reaching adulthood. In reality, this liberty was given to them that they might realize in human society a type of man and woman whose personalities would be integrated into the realities of faith. Those who fail, blame their failure on the fact that they were cut off from the world, while the real reason is that they never accepted the absolute quality of faith-realities. Their faith was too feeble to enable them to live at any deep level, and also too weak to give true meaning to human values.

What truly constitutes a personality is not the fact of being submerged in human reality, but the ability to give a meaning to that reality, the ability to master it and to express it either by one's life or by one's work. On the other hand, reality destroys the person incapable of making a choice, turning him into a robot. But he whom an ideal inspires, who has a task in view, places himself right in the center of that reality and gives it direction. Here lies the human personality's power to assume responsibility. The stronger the personality is, the greater will be its power to unify. And what enables it to take hold of itself, to form itself, is a project or a task which cannot be realized unless that personality polarize all its energies. A man remains undeveloped then, half-identified and without adult status, until the day he makes a decision which is capable of orienting his entire existence.

In the case of a minor short-term project, absorbing only a part of my life, it is not necessary that the motivation be as deep or as absolute as in the case of a project engaging my entire existence. I can, for example, postpone the date of my wedding in order to be able to realize with greater freedom a project I may have on hand, but the more the project is linked to my total existence, the more it ought to demand of my time and energies and the deeper ought to be its motivation. Similarly, it may so happen that the motivation is of such depth that it demands the gift of my entire life. There is consequently an intimate relationship between depth and duration. That is why a love that is real can only be conceived as eternal, engaging as it does the entire being in its every dimension.

Here we find the meaning of life-engagement in religious celibacy. Only that which is perpetual *can speak to the infinite depths*. If human love demands a "forever," how much more divine love, which touches us at still greater depths.

If human love helps these who love each other to grow into adulthood, why can divine love not do likewise? If divine love does not succeed in making an adult out of a particular person, it is because that person does not cooperate with God's action. Divine love is no abstract thing. It is a love that is real and that fulfills us just as does every other love. It is light. It moves us. It is also warmth. It makes us active and capable of accepting difficult challenge. Divine love's source is beyond this world; but when it reveals itself, it passes through our subconscious, through our feelings, indeed through our entire humanity, but it differs from human love in its origin and in its final goal. It expresses itself in and by the purest human love, but at the same time it reveals itself as a visitor from a world beyond human love, and directs us toward a love that no heart can contain and no word can describe.

Thus it is that divine love becomes one of the most powerful agents in the growth of a human personality. Christ and the saints of every religion are proof of this. Must our present age be deprived of this treasure which is the integration in the human person of the gift of nature and of grace? It is perhaps more difficult for one who is a "eunuch for the kingdom of heaven" to achieve adult status than it is for the married person, and yet I hesitate to make a definite statement here. This maturity integrates elements which are different from those integrated by the married person, and vice versa. They are but two ways of being a man, and humanity is just as much in need of the one as of the other.

Chapter 28

For Today and for Tomorrow

Survey after survey has been made to ascertain whether or not priests ought to marry. Does this mean that, according to the results of such surveys, the Church will eventually abolish compulsory celibacy for the priesthood? I very much doubt it, if she holds to the spirit of her Founder, who after all did not come to propose an ideal corresponding to the desires of the majority. In proposing that of celibacy for the kingdom, He made no secret of the fact that very few were capable of understanding its meaning. He would say the very same today. Christ fulfilled the Law in transcending it and thus in abolishing it. He did away with the institutional priesthood so as to inaugurate a priesthood that would be entirely new. To say, however, that every member of God's people is a priest is to resolve only one part of the problem, for we see Christ form around Him a small group of disciples and an even smaller group of apostles. These are destined to be His witnesses in a special way. Let us admit that we have not as yet found the solution to the problem of the Christian priesthood, but let us not be too ready to claim that the ministry ought to be reduced to a function, while ceasing to be a charism.

In this troubled world, old men have visions and young men

dream dreams. These children are adults going through an "adolescence" crisis and in search of their identity at the age of 40. They leave the celibate life and pursue their marriage dream. The old men are those who project into the future their happy past, as though nothing should change. Instead of projecting onto the screen of the future our desires of our past existence, let us face the problem in a concrete fashion. Is there a place in today's world, and in that of tomorrow, for the celibate?

It is said far too often that when one understands the grandeur of marriage, celibacy loses all its meaning. When a person is suffering from the solitude inevitable in celibate life, marriage can, it is true, seem to be the solution to all problems. In marriage, one can love, find fulfillment, realize one's existence. It is true that, when compared to unhappiness in celibacy, marriage is heaven. But how many married people also envy—at least at certain moments—those who are celibate! If it is true that many priests and religious men and women have found the fulfillment they longed for in marriage, how many others have found in it nothing but solitude and frustration. We should not forget this side of the·problem, when the question arises as to what value celibacy can have for today and for tomorrow.

It is a fact that cannot be denied that many took a false step in choosing a celibate life. But that celibacy is no longer meaningful and that tomorrow's priests should be married—that's another question! As I said already, Christ did not link celibacy to priesthood, but He did better still. He Himself appeared as a celibate, or in more energetic language still, as a eunuch. He could say, when speaking of Himself and of His apostles: "Yes, we are eunuchs, and we know why." He had no wish to place Himself on purely legalistic ground. He just said: "He who can understand, let him understand." He did not say: "If you really want to be my disciple, abstain from marriage." What He did say, in order to express clearly what His wishes were, was: "If you are thinking of a wife, give up the idea." This saying is hard, but the Lord did say this several times. And yet here again, there is no question of imposing anything. Rather, He proposes.

Christ's proposition remains valid for today as it does for tomorrow. We must not be surprised because it shocks people. If the world chooses to believe that celibacy is impossible, that is its affair. Christ lived the celibate life, and so did His apostles; and it is with these same apostles that He shared His thoughts. During His lifetime, He manifested Himself in an intimate way to several persons, to Martha and Mary, to Nicodemus, and to many others. Yet it is to this intimate group whom we call apostles that He gave His message.

Was it not such witnesses that Christ wished for! He drew them into the mystery of His friendship that they might give testimony to His human and divine reality. Have we not here the ideal type of witnesses whom Christ wished to leave behind after His ascension? Why would not he whom we designate "priest" be defined first and foremost as the "witness" to the mystery of God revealed to our world? It is here that the gospel seems to me compelling: Christ's privileged witnesses were those whom He initiated in a special way into His mystery, those whom He called apostles, because they had left all behind in order to follow Him.

The understanding of things divine is the work of the Holy Spirit. When Christ left this world, He promised to send His Spirit. This He did, and this same Spirit has ceaselessly inspired men and women to leave all things and to renounce marriage for the love of Christ and their fellowmen. However, the battle between the Spirit and what St. John calls the world will go on till the end of time. The world hates the celibate because in its eyes he is incomprehensible. And yet, in the Church, the Spirit will continue to inspire men and women to follow the way of virginity.

In a world that rejects institutions, refuses conformity, and aspires after true freedom, the Spirit seeks expression. Now celibacy is a victory for the Spirit. He testifies that real love, human or divine, is to be sought in the depths of the human being, beyond everything that is carnal. He reveals to surprised and incredulous men that God is love and that He can inspire in human beings the desire to renounce married love in order to live here below, in the concrete conditions of human existence, the love of Him who is love. Finally, the Spirit reveals that, however divine this love be, it has the power of enriching in a wonderful manner those who yield themselves to its power. This mystical response to the love of God is without doubt what has given to humanity some of its greatest representatives. Must we deprive our own age and the age yet to come of that divine richness shining through the features of men's faces!